# They All Were Looking for a King...

*Cycle C Sermons for Advent/Christmas/Epiphany Based on the Gospel Texts*

Wayne Brouwer

CSS Publishing Company, Inc.
Lima, Ohio

THEY ALL WERE LOOKING FOR A KING...

FIRST EDITION
Copyright © 2012
by CSS Publishing Co., Inc.

Published by CSS Publishing Company, Inc., Lima, Ohio 45807. All rights reserved. No part of this publication may be reproduced in any manner whatsoever without the prior permission of the publisher, except in the case of brief quotations embodied in critical articles and reviews. Inquiries should be addressed to: CSS Publishing Company, Inc., Permissions Department, 5450 N. Dixie Highway, Lima, Ohio 45807.

Scripture quotations are from the New Revised Standard Version of the Bible. Copyright 1989 by the Division of Christian Education of the National Council of the Churches of Christ in the USA. Used by permission.

---

**Library of Congress Cataloging-in-Publication Data**

Brouwer, Wayne, 1954-
  They all were looking for a King-- : Cycle C, sermons for Advent, Christmas, Epiphany : based on the Gospel texts / Wayne Brouwer. -- 1st ed.
      p. cm.
  Includes bibliographical references and index.
  1. Bible. N.T. Gospels--Sermons. 2. Advent sermons. 3. Christmas sermons. 4. Epiphany--Sermons. 5. Church year sermons. 6. Common lectionary (1992). Year C. I. Title.

  BS2555.54.B77 2012
  252'.61--dc23
                                                           2012005044

---

For more information about CSS Publishing Company resources, visit our website at www.csspub.com, email us at csr@csspub.com, or call (800) 241-4056.

ISBN-13: 978-0-7880-2681-2
ISBN-10: 0-7880-2681-X                           PRINTED IN USA

*For my Western Theological students
who endured the cross (of Greek)
to gain the victory!*

# Table of Contents

**Preface**   7

**Advent 1**   9
   A Cry in the Dark
   Luke 21:25-36

**Advent 2**   15
   The Peaceable Kingdom
   Luke 3:1-6

**Advent 3**   21
   A Dance in the Desert
   Luke 3:7-18

**Advent 4**   31
   King Jesus
   Luke 1:39-45 (46-55)

**Christmas Eve / Day**   39
   The Wrong Gift
   Luke 2:1-14 (15-20)

**Christmas 1**   49
   In Praise of Praise
   Luke 2:41-52

**New Year's Day**   53
   At the Gate of the Year
   Matthew 25:31-46

**Epiphany of Our Lord**   63
   Shine, Jesus, Shine!
   Matthew 2:1-12

**Baptism of Our Lord** 73
**Epiphany 1**
**Ordinary Time 1**
    Here Comes Jesus!
    Luke 3:15-17, 21-22

**Epiphany 2** 77
**Ordinary Time 2**
    Becoming What We Were Meant to Be
    John 2:1-11

**Epiphany 3** 83
**Ordinary Time 3**
    Creating Community the Hard Way
    Luke 4:14-21

**Epiphany 4** 89
**Ordinary Time 4**
    Prophet
    Luke 4:21-30

**Transfiguration of Our Lord** 95
**(Last Sunday after Epiphany)**
    Glow in the Dark
    Luke 9:28-36 (37-43)

**If You Like This Title...** 103

# *Preface*

*They all were looking for a king
To slay their foes and lift them high;
Thou cam'st a little Baby thing
That made a woman cry.*

*O Son of Man, to right my lot
Naught but Thy presence can avail;
Yet on the road Thy wheels are not,
Nor on the sea Thy sail.*

*My fancied ways why should'st Thou heed?
Thou com'st down Thine own secret stair;
Com'st down to answer all my need,
Yes, every bygone prayer.*
— "They All Were Looking for a King"
George MacDonald, 1883 (public domain)

George MacDonald wrote this poem for friends: friends of his, and friends of Jesus. We own it, too, because George MacDonald believed, through his "romantic theology," that God truly wanted all of us to become friends through Jesus. There is a relational directness and simplicity about George MacDonald's religious perspectives that is built upon story. One of the "Inklings" with C.S. Lewis, J.R.R. Tolkien, and Dorothy Sayers, MacDonald loved to tell stories. The most fascinating of all stories, for him, was that of God's love affair with us. MacDonald was passionate about it and retold it in a thousand different ways.

Of course, the source of this great narrative is found in the gospels of the New Testament. As the common lectionary pulls us anew into the story that is much larger than ourselves, but in which we become very important, we rehearse again the words and ways of Jesus. With MacDonald we seek much and find deceptively more in the grace of Jesus, even though it comes to us in ways we never imagined.

— Wayne Brouwer

**Advent 1**
**Luke 21:25-36**

# A Cry in the Dark

"Screw your courage to the sticking-place," says Lady Macbeth to her doomed husband in Shakespeare's tragedy, "and we'll not fail." But fail they do and no amount of courage in the world can save them or turn them into heroes.

Courage is a funny thing. It's a bit like happiness: the more you seek it, the more you demand it, the more you try to call it up, the less it shows its face.

Words can stir us to courage but only when they are grounded in confident expectation and hitched to unshakable values or realities. Who would not rally around the "I have a dream…" speech delivered by Martin Luther King Jr., in which he paints the colors of freedom? Who would not feel stronger listening to the dogged determination of Winston Churchill in the dark days of 1940: "Let us… brace ourselves to our duty, and so bear ourselves that, if the British Empire and its Commonwealth last for a thousand years, men will still say, 'This was their finest hour!'"

Courage, as faith's activator, is the call in Jesus' words to us today. He sits with his shell-shocked disciples in the temple precincts, sensing the profound disturbance at his words that this marvelous place of holiness and beauty will soon lie in rubble, but pointing them to a larger cataclysm that will shake the whole earth as eternity finally sears into time.

We've been there with the disciples, haven't we? Famed psychiatrist Viktor Frankl remembered a terrible day during World War II. He was on a work gang, just outside the fences that hid the horrors of Hitler's infamous Dachau death camp. "We were at work in a trench," wrote Frankl. "The dawn was gray around us; gray was the sky above; gray the snow in the pale light of dawn; gray rags in which my fellow prisoners were clad, and gray their faces."

Frankl tells how he was ready to die. It was as if the gray bleakness had claws and each moment they dug deeper and colder into his soul. Why go on? What could be the purpose in "living" if, indeed, he was even still alive at this moment? There was no heaven, no hell, no future, no past. Only the clutching grayness of this miserable moment.

Suddenly, to his surprise, Frankl felt "a last violent protest" surging within himself. He sensed that even though his body had given up and his mind had accepted defeat, his inner spirit was taking flight. It was searching. It was looking. It was scanning the eternal horizons for the faintest glimmer that said his fleeting life had some divine purpose. It was looking for God.

In a single instant two things happened, says Frankl, that simply could not be mere coincidence. Within, he heard a powerful cry, piercing the gloom and tearing at the icy claws of death. The voice shouted "Yes!" against the "No" of defeat and the gray "I don't know" of the moment.

At that exact second, "a light was lit in a distant farmhouse." Like a beacon it called attention to itself. It spoke of life, warmth, family, and love. Frankl said that in that moment he began to believe. And in that moment he began to live again.

Advent often reminds us of our similar need. The grayness of our bleak days is stifling. The loneliness of the moment overwhelms us. Is there a reason to carry on? Is there meaning beyond the drudgery of today's repetitive struggles? Is there hope and is there God?

With David (Psalm 43:3), we shout, "Send out your light and your truth!" Don't leave me alone. Give me some sign. Light a candle in the window and take me home.

Advent reminds us of the power in Jesus' words to his disciples. God never denies us the light we need. As Joyce Kilmer wrote:

> *Because the road was steep and long,*
> *and through a dark and lonely land,*
> *God set upon my lips a song*
> *and put a lantern in my hand.*
> — Albert Joyce Kilmer, "Love's Lantern" (public domain)

Still, sometimes it seems there's no getting away from a bad thing. In the mid-1800s, Dutch immigrant pastor and community leader Albertus Van Raalte watched his little colony in western Michigan disintegrate under the ravages of disease and death. One Sunday morning, in the middle of his congregational prayer, he broke down. Sobbing and throwing his hands toward the heavens, he shouted, "Oh God! Must we all die?"

Certainly there are times when each of us goes through that agony. It's one thing to experience trouble and torment when you've been living an ungodly existence. You know that you're getting what you deserve. But it's quite another thing to be close to God and still to feel such pain and frustration each day. The specter of death bumps against us in the marketplace. If we run for cover, it follows us right into the caves of refuge. Too often we wear Van Raalte's tear-stained cheeks and swollen eyes, shouting toward heaven, "Oh God! Is there no relief?"

Because we know these pressures, there is something absolutely amazing about the strength, peace, and confidence that are part of our return to Advent anticipations. We need to remember again the fundamental secret to living on the edge of cruelty, pain, spite, injury, and death. We need to learn anew that only a God who has ultimate control over all these things can make life itself meaningful. Only a God who allows the miseries for a time — as a parent might restrain a helping hand so that a child can grow through the struggles of development — can finally bring all things into his larger plans for peace, joy, and harmony.

There is a powerful scene in Herman Melville's great epic, *Moby Dick*, where Captain Ahab stands peg-legged on the deck of the *Pequod* during a violent storm (ch. 119). His obsession with the white whale has carried the craft and crew to exotic and frightening locales, and now it seems as if divine providence might be unleashing furious anger against this ill-fated quest. But Ahab is a fighter, and with clenched fists, amid the lightning bolts and against the raging thunder he yells a taunt at the Creator who chastens his cause: "I now know thee, thou clear spirit, and I now know that thy right worship is defiance."

Yet even Captain Ahab, torn by his demons and captured as much by the whale as he seeks to capture it, knows that there is a need greater than victory and a power more tenacious than brutal force. He falls to the deck in a tormented confession: "But war is pain, and hate is woe. Come in thy lowest form of love, and I will kneel and kiss thee...." He almost pleads with God to stop the awful battering of antagonistic powers and descend in kind humility so that the passions of love might be reborn and rekindled again.

This, of course, is a marvelous bridge between the bellicose prophecies of the Old Testament and the juxtaposed incarnation of Jesus that emerged out of them. God did indeed come down, like God had done in the times of Moses and the Pharaoh. But this time God chose the suckling child rather than the plague blasts as the means of arrival and encounter. We who marshal our forces for good or for evil are suddenly caught up short — the one who could "rend the heavens" and "set twigs ablaze" and "cause water to boil" and "cause the nations to quake" and "make the mountains tremble" slipped in as a helpless child, and the world knelt to kiss him on a starry night in Bethlehem.

This is the language of Advent, the renewed language of confidence in God, the crisis of these times, and the anticipated next act of divine intervention in human affairs. But it all begins with the faithfulness of God upon which our own faith and faithfulness can be pinned.

Advent is, for the church, a solid hook in the vast, uncharted chaotic voids of space, allowing us to tether and take our bearings from at least one point which is neither shifting with the currents nor dependent on our own powers to establish it. Advent is the place where Archimedes can set the fulcrum of his lever and move earth and the planets in a meaningful way because there is a critical unmoved position from which everything else is to be measured. Advent is a date on our calendars that was penned in by God, not us, indicating a promised encounter we might often doubt but it cannot be erased from the pages of time.

We once promised one of our daughters that we would visit her, over 5,000 miles away from where we live, at a certain date in the future. She counted on our arrival and made plans to greet us, house us, feed us, and show us around her world. How could she be so certain that we would be there when we promised? Because she knows our character. She has learned to trust us and trust in us. True, the "fickle finger of fate" might raise all manner of obstacles and perhaps even void our plans, but not if we could help it. Our word is as good as gold with our daughter. She trusts us. She was confident we would be there. She arranged her life by that promise.

How much more should we expect God to keep promises? In the spare evidence of these days, when we are roiled by circumstances and challenged by materialistic denials of any first cause, religious trust seems foolish. Except... except that God made a promise. And we have seen God's character in creation and in the divine affairs with Israel and in the testimony of Jesus. So we wait… Amen.

**Advent 2**
**Luke 3:1-6**

# *The Peaceable Kingdom*

What difference does my life make for others around me? What difference does anyone's life make? It's always a question related to parenting. Parents make choices that affect the manner in which their children form their identities. Harry Chapin put it well in his song, "Cat's in the Cradle." When he was a young father he was too busy making a living to be bothered by his son. When he was finally old enough to enjoy time with the family, his son had learned to be too busy for him!

Of course, the other side of the story is just as true. Maurice Boyd remembers the impact of one incident that sealed the impact of his father on his life forever. His father worked in a shipyard in Belfast, Ireland. During the Depression, work dried up. Times were tough and for three years his father was out of a job.

Then one of his old bosses at the shipyard approached his father. The important man would find work for Mr. Boyd. He would guarantee it, no matter how much worse things got. All Mr. Boyd would have to do would be to buy a life-insurance policy from the man. It would work to their mutual benefit: the boss' income would increase, and Mr. Boyd's work income would be guaranteed!

It was a great deal except for one thing: it was illegal. Maurice Boyd remembers his father sitting at the kitchen table with the whole family surrounding him. There at the table his father counted the cost. He reviewed their desperate financial situation. He ticked off the outstanding bills, and the money he ought to be making — could be making — if only he'd say yes to his boss.

His father wrote it all down on a sheet of paper: the gains and the losses; what he could make and what he could lose. Then he wrote down a category that Maurice Boyd will never forget: integrity! What did it matter if he gained the cash to pay the rent but lost his ability to teach his children right from wrong? What did it matter if he gained the dignity of a job, but lost it each morning when he looked at himself in the mirror and knew that the only reason he can go to work instead of someone else is because he cheated? Says Maurice Boyd: "He discovered that no one can make you feel inferior without your consent and that one way you can keep your soul is by refusing to sell it. He realized that whatever else he lost, and God knows he lost enough, he didn't have to lose himself."

John the Baptist shouted that message to the crowds from Jerusalem who came to see his odd ministry at the Jordan River. The hardest thing to do in life is to maintain our integrity. Sin has entered the human soul precisely at this point. We are not, most of us, evil people. We're rather nice, aren't we? There's much that we do that's good, fine, noble, kind, and wise, and no one can deny that.

Here's the problem: Whatever else sin might do in our lives, it first and foremost perforates the lines of our hearts and lets us tear off a piece here and a piece there until we find ourselves segmented, fragmented, torn apart in separate snippets of self. It isn't that we become blackened by sin in one large stroke. It isn't that we turn into hideous monsters of greed and cruelty. It isn't that we dissolve the Dr. Jekylls of our personalities into dastardly Mr. Hydes. Instead, we keep most of our goodness intact, but we make small allowances in certain little areas. We cheat on our taxes a little, maybe… Or we turn our eyes from the needs of someone we could help... Or we compromise our communication until we speak from only our mouths instead of our souls.

The fragmentation of our lives makes us less than we should be, less than we could be. It makes us less than the people God made us to be. It is precisely because we and our world have lost our integrity that the great prophet of God must come and set things right.

There is a powerful scene in Robert Bolt's play *A Man for All Seasons*. The story is that of Sir Thomas More, loyal subject of the English crown. King Henry VIII wants to change things to suit his own devious plans, so he requires all his nobles to swear an oath of allegiance that violates the conscience of Sir Thomas More before his God. Since he will not swear the oath, More is put in jail. His daughter Margaret comes to visit him. "Meg," he calls her, with affection. She's his pride and joy, the one who thinks his thoughts after him.

Meg comes to plead with her father in prison. "Take the oath, Father!" she urges him. "Take it with your mouth, if you can't take it with your heart! Take it and return to us! You can't do us any good in here! And you can't be there for us if the king should execute you!"

She's right in so many ways! Yet her father answers her this way: "Meg, when a man swears an oath, he holds himself in his hands like water, and if he opens his fingers, how can he hope to find himself again?"

You know what he means, don't you? When our lives begin to fragment, it's like holding our lives like water in our hands, and then letting our fingers come apart, just a little bit. The water of our very selves dribbles away. We may look like the same people, but who we are inside has begun to change.

This is why John comes pointing the way to another kingdom. Here there will be no separation between the impulse of the heart, the thought of the mind, the word of the mouth, and the action of the hands. Somehow, everything about the coming kingdom is integrated. That's the meaning of the word "integrity," isn't it? Pure in heart!

When the one of integrity arrives, this world must change. This is why we celebrate Advent over and over, until the coming again of God's anointed one. When Bill Moyers interviewed Dr. Rachel Naomi Remen, she told him how it was for her. Dr. Remen has founded several institutes for the care of cancer patients. She said that sometimes she has a much greater sense of integrity during those times when she isn't feeling all that well physically. Bill asked her what she meant by "integrity," and she replied, "That I am what I am…" She said that even with her wounds and her weaknesses, "there's an essence and a uniqueness and a beauty" about her life that is whole and complete. Integrity. Pure in heart. The peaceable kingdom.

Jesus raises the banner of heaven's royal claims over Gentile and Jewish territory, and thus is the source of political allegiances that supersede temporal boundaries. This is very good news during Advent, when the nations of the earth conspire against one another, and only the Christian church can effect a transnational celebration of the politics of grace. The peaceable kingdom.

Robert Coles is a child psychiatrist and professor at Harvard University who likes to figure out why we do the things we do. In his book *The Call of Service* he wonders about people who try to make a difference in life. People who seek to reform themselves, even with the tenacity of sin that clings down deep. People who attempt to better society, in spite of the fact that it stubbornly refuses the challenge.

Why do they do it? Coles asks. The stories are all so different that it is hard to figure out a way to summarize them neatly in some framework. In fact, the people themselves often have a hard time defining what it is that makes them tick. One young teacher in an urban school is challenged all the time. Street-smart students, weary of self-righteous "do-gooders," put the question to him. "What's in it for you?" they demand. And he really can't say.

But this he and all the rest of them can say: Sometime earlier in their lives, each of them ran into a crisis situation, a situation that tested their identity and their willingness to do something about it, and in that crisis situation, each of them encountered someone who put his life on the line. Someone who taught them the meaning of service. Someone who gave of herself in a way that bucks the trend of selfishness and self-preservation. And the influence of that someone else made it possible to be greater than each of them had previously considered. Enter the peaceable kingdom, where things change because we have brushed against the holiness of God, and Jesus becomes our Savior and mentor.

Years ago, when radio station WXYZ in Detroit was the big news in broadcasting, people spent hours each night listening to the latest episodes of "The Green Hornet," and "Sergeant Preston of the Yukon." Nearly every year the station brought out a new dramatic hero.

Station manager George Trendle often suggested the main ideas for these characters. In fact, he was the inspiration behind one of the most famous figures they ever created: The Lone Ranger. Trendle said this about the man he had in mind: "He's a sober-minded man with a righteous purpose to make kids look up to him."

But that's easily lost on us. When Thomas Naylor was teaching business management at Duke University, he asked his students to draft a personal strategic plan. He reports that "with few exceptions, what they wanted fell into three categories: money, power, and things — very big things."

In fact, said Naylor, this was their request of the business faculty at Duke University: "Teach me to be a money-making machine!" A money-making machine! A machine with no heart! That's the fragmentation of our lives taken to the extreme.

So here we are, in a sense, on the brink of another year, the liturgical year, the year of expectation of God's doing something good once again, the year of the coming of the kingdom announced by John. As they say, "Today is the first day of the rest of your life!" Let's imagine that there are 365 new days thrown back onto the credits side of the ledger. What do we do with them? Each day in the year ahead 9,077 babies will be born; 2,740 young people will run away from home; 63,288 traffic accidents will occur, in which 129 people will die; 5,962 couples will get married and 1,986 will divorce; 500 million cups of coffee will be drank; and the snack bars at O'Hare Airport in Chicago will sell 5,479 hot dogs.

And each of us will be challenged in one of the three great crises of life:

> The Identity Crisis: Who am I?
> The Influence Crisis: What does my life mean to those around me?
> The Integrity Crisis: How deep is my soul?

Do we know the hope of the coming kingdom and the one who has the capacity to restore our integrity because of his own? Amen.

**Advent 3**
**Luke 3:7-18**

# *A Dance in the Desert*

Even though we like laughter and enjoy praise and celebration, especially at this time of year, it doesn't always come easily. One fellow tells of his work as a hospital volunteer. He couldn't believe the pain and suffering he saw there: burn victims, deformities, terminal cancer. He watched the little ones cry. Some children were so lonely. Their parents couldn't take the trauma, so they never came to visit their own children. How horrible!

This fellow decided to get a clown's nose and a pair of oversized shoes. Then he painted his face and pulled on a wig. When he went to work dressed like that the next day, some of the children were scared, some were captivated, and some even showed hints of a smile for the first time in ages.

But others couldn't stop wailing. They were consumed by agony. What could he do for them? The next day the clown brought along some popcorn. When he came to the side of a crying child, he took a kernel of popcorn, placed it against the child's cheek, and soaked up the cascading tears with its fluff. Then he popped that kernel into his mouth and ate it.

It was a stroke of genius. The only time some of those children stopped crying was the moment they knew somebody else cared enough to swallow their tears.

Advent brings us to a place like that. It takes us, at the end of our journey, to the "sanctuary" of God for a time of praise. "Sanctuary" is refuge, fortress, safe house, security, arms of love, a place where someone cares enough to swallow our tears and protect us from the worst that could harm us.

Madeleine L'Engle paints a picture of such a sanctuary in one of her children's books. She tells of a young couple on a desert journey through wilderness in a rough caravan. They're on their way to Egypt. Someone is after them; someone wants to kill their little boy.

The journey is a rugged one. The desert is alive with ferocious beasts. All eyes cast about uneasily as darkness settles. There'll be little sleep in the camp tonight. They build a great fire to drive back the shadows and keep away the world that belongs to monsters with glowing eyes. Suddenly they start in terror; a great lion appears at the bonfire. The mother reaches for her child, desperately trying to draw him to safety.

But the child stands and laughs. He opens his arms wide to the lion. The lion lifts his front paws and hops around on his hind legs. He's dancing! Then, from the desert, come running several little mice, two donkeys, a snake, and a couple of clumsy ostriches. Three great eagles swoop in from the purple skies and from the other side of the camp a unicorn emerges, a pelican, and even two dragons.

They all bow before the child and then dance together, round and round him. He stands at the center of their great circle, laughing in delight. It's a dance in the desert, as L'Engle calls it. In essence, it's the sum and substance of our worship here on earth, pilgrims passing through the wilderness of ghastly beasties and mournful hurts.

This is the third Sunday in Advent. Christmas seems close, but we are not there yet. We still spend time in the dark alongside those who wrestle with demons and shadows and beasties. Because of Advent confidence, we see the light and clap our hands in celebration of the child who comes to dance around our fires.

A young girl was watching a parade with her parents when the Scottish Bagpipe Band came by. As her dad explained how the pipes worked, pointing to the bags under the arms of the players, the girl put her hands over her ears and shouted above the shrill sound, "Maybe if they stop squeezing, the bags will stop screaming!"

Sometimes we avoid the biblical prophets because all we hear is their piercing jeremiads. Yet if we take the time to meet them in their historical context, the prophets bring us back to divine messages we desperately need. There is an inherent consistency of message and focus among all of these diverse religious ruminations and rantings. First of all, the prophetic sermons are invariably rooted in the web of relationships created by the Sinai Covenant. Israel belongs to Yahweh and her lifestyle must be shaped by the stipulations of that suzerain-vassal treaty. Obedience to Yahweh triggers the blessings of the Sinai Covenant, while disobedience is the first reason for Israel's experiences of its curses — drought, war, famine, enemy occupation, destruction of cities and fields, deportation, and so on. For this reason the prophetic writings are laced with moral diatribes that carry a strong emphasis on social ethics.

Second, the function and message of prophecy was very political. For Israel to come under the domination of other nations was always seen as a divine scourge resulting from the application of the covenant curses because of Israel's disobedience. How Israel handled its international relations showed plainly whether she trusted Yahweh or had otherwise become enamored with power and politics rooted in lesser gods. Constantly the prophets asked whether Israel was Yahweh's witnessing people, or if she was merely another nation with no particular mission or divine purpose. Israel's self-understanding was always very religious and at the same time very political.

Third, as the epochs of Israel's political fortunes unfolded, the message of the prophets became increasingly apocalyptic. There was a growing sense that because things had not gone the way they should have, producing heartfelt and on-going national repentance and covenant restoration, Yahweh will have to intervene directly again, in a manner similar to that which happened during the time of Moses. When Yahweh interrupts human history the next time, however, along with judgments on the wickedness of the nations of the world, Israel will also fall heavily under divine punishment. Because Yahweh is on a mission to restore the fallen world, this next major divine intervention will be paired with a focus also on establishing a new world order, even as the old is falling away under the conflagration. In this coming messianic age, everything in society and the natural realm will finally function in the manner the Creator had intended in the beginning. Furthermore, because Yahweh is faithful to promises made, Israel will not be forgotten and a remnant of God's servant nation will be at the center of all this renewal, restoration, and great joy.

This increasingly forward-looking thrust of prophecy leads some to think of it as primarily foretelling, a kind of crystal ball gaze into the future. In reality, however, the nature of prophecy in ancient Israel is more forth-telling, declaring again the meaning of the ancient Sinai Covenant, explaining the mission of Yahweh as witness to the world, and describing the implications of the morality envisioned by the suzerain-vassal treaty stipulations.

By the time the seventh century BC rolled around, the prophets were rarely welcome in the royal palaces, even though all that was left of a once proud and expansive Israel was the tiny mountainous territory of Judah. During the 600s, although Assyria kept threatening Jerusalem, it was increasingly occupied in defending itself against its rebellious eastern province of Babylon. During these years, while

Jeremiah developed his gloomy diatribes in the heart of the capital city, Zephaniah (630-610 BC) provided a few paragraphs against Judah and the nations that surrounded it (chs. 1-2), couching the imminent intervention of Yahweh in the increasingly common term, "The Day of the Lord." In this final chapter, Zephaniah turned his attention toward restoration and renewal, pointing to a future when the fortunes of Yahweh's people would be made full once again. His words are the basis for all Advent celebrations: in a darkened world where the ways of God are no longer known, God will rescue the covenant community, restore their joys, and provide a light of grace that shines through them, beckoning the nations to enter the messianic celebration with them.

The true light, of course, would be Jesus, even though Zephaniah could not have understood at the time exactly how the divine message through him would be fulfilled. We, on the third Sunday of Advent, know exactly what God had in mind and now wait in expectation for Jesus' culminating return to fully and perfectly realize the grandeur of the messianic kingdom. Someday the prophetic bagpipes will no longer be squeezed, and the music of the angels will shout the "Hallelujah" chorus.

One of the great words of Advent is joy. It is a constant theme of the prophets when characterizing the redeemed community that emerges from exile and awaits God's next and greatest act. It is the heartbeat of Elizabeth and Zachariah as they hear that their cursed infertility is giving way to the medical impossibility of God's special pregnancy. It is the incredulous lyric of Mary's song as she feels the miracle of God's love growing inside her. Joy is the primary category in the index of the hymns of the church.

Joy is also a slippery eel, often squeezing past our best laid religious trappings and devotional weapons. In the East, the story is told of an extremely wealthy king who ruled a vast domain from magnificent palaces. He had the respect of his citizens and peace within his borders. Yet for some perplexing reason he was very unhappy. The king's doctors could find no medical problem. Neither could psychiatrists figure it out. One old wise man finally provided this advice: "There is but a single cure for the king. Your majesty must sleep for one night wearing the shirt of a truly happy man."

Strange advice, to be sure! But the desperate king needed only a hint of finding release from his malady to command that the search begin. So his messengers scoured the land, looking for one truly happy person.

Tragically, they couldn't find even one happy person! Everyone had experienced days of sorrow and times of mourning. Many might laugh for a moment but sooner or later each person would settle back to reflect on the pain in his or her life.

Almost beyond hope, the messengers suddenly happened upon a beggar next to the road leading back to the palace. He wore a smile. He giggled uncontrollably. He laughed at life as it surrounded him. Here was a truly happy man!

"Give us your shirt," the messengers demanded. "The king has need of it!"

But the fellow only doubled over with spasms of hilarity. "I'm sorry!" he gasped, between fits of laughter. "I have no shirt!"

Tantalizing, isn't it? To see joy and not to own it? To hear laughter and yet to find your own throat stopped with pain and silence? To have a cure within hand's reach and still missing the opportunity to close the deal? But that's where Advent joy is such a great message of the "good news" of the church, especially in the darkness of sin's night and earth's blight. For Paul, it is the essential word to speak and to live, so much so that he has to repeat himself about it.

The English language has a number of similar words that relate to good feelings inside. Pleasure, for instance, reflects our delighted response to sensations that stimulate us.

Happiness surrounds us because of certain happenings in our lives. And then there's joy.

In a sense, pleasure is an "it" word; it mostly has to do with things that touch our senses. And happiness is a "me" word; its primary focus is my response to events that come and go in my life. But joy is really a "we" word; it usually reflects what happens between persons, between me and you, between me and God.

Joy, as Paul notes in his letter to the Philippians, starts in the heart. It's a relational word. Rejoice in the Lord. Robert Rainy, one-time head of New College in Edinburgh, Scotland, used to say that "joy is the flag which is flown from the castle of the heart when the king is in residence there!"

If joy starts in the heart, it is refined in the mind. It is more than an emotion that comes and goes. It is deeper than a reflexive response that needs the right kind of stimulation. It is an act of the will. "I will say it again: rejoice!" commands Paul in his letter to the Philippian Christians. Joy grows from heartfelt relationships. But it is also a choice of the mind, as John makes clear when he applies this treatment to those who come to him looking for a way beyond the humdrum of their lives. Joy must be chosen as a part of sealing the deal, and joy comes when we direct our attention to serving others.

John seems to have had all the charisma of a pit bull or a nightclub bouncer. He looked strange. He had no time for conversational pleasantries. He didn't use Dale Carnegie's techniques to "win friends and influence people." The only word was slicingly divisive; the only message a stab through the heart. "You brood of vipers!" he harangued his fans and paparazzi, yelling at them that neither bloodlines nor cultural heritage nor religious piety gave them a leg up in life.

But for John, the bad news is good news, and the good news only sneaks in on the shoulders of the bad. As another John ("of the cross") would later remind us, it is only when we pass through the "dark night of the soul" that we are finally ready for dawn, aching for its energies to transform the world in which we have wallowed too long.

John was a larger-than-life figure in himself and his public interactions, yet he was surprisingly self-effacive. While the crowds flocked to hear him preach, mesmerized by his one-note song played with sirenic intrigue, his finger kept pointing in another direction. "I'm not the one!" he cried. "Look to him who follows me!" he shouted. "Stake your claim in that one's field!"

Of course, what John expected from his cousin was an even larger troll to rain more tar and feathers on polite society. "I baptized you with water," John warned, "but he will consume you with fire!"

John was the last of the Old Testament prophets, a transitional figure like Samuel of old, standing between the judges and the kings. John could sing Barry McGuire's "Eve of Destruction" better than that raspy-voiced seer of the American Cultural Revolution ever would. John realized that tectonic plates were colliding, the old order was passing more quickly than a Bob Dylan song, and few would enter the New Age of Messiah unless they passed first through the fires of judgment.

But that is exactly what made him the talk of the town in first-century Jerusalem. As another namesake (John Wesley) put it, when they asked him why people came to hear him preach, "The Holy Spirit sets my heart on fire, and folks show up just to watch me burn!" John was the doomsday prophet par excellence. He had decoded the secrets of the Old Testament and realized he was standing on the brink of the New. What would happen next, he was not entirely certain, but whatever it was, people should not presume to drift blithely from one into the other. When God slams into our world to deal with our stuff, no one can expect him to play nice.

On this third Sunday of Advent, it is not Santa Claus we are looking for, and John knew it. Jesus once slipped into our world by the backdoor. It won't happen the same way next time. There is much to hope for, to be sure, but it's a fire walk designed to scare the hell out of everyone that marks the path into the eternal kingdom. Listen to John. Amen.

**Advent 4**
**Luke 1:39-45 (46-55)**

# *King Jesus*

One morning in 1872, David Livingstone wrote this in his diary: "March 19, my birthday. My Jesus, my king, my life, my all, I again dedicate my whole self to thee. Accept me, and grant, O gracious Father, that ere the year is gone I may finish my work. In Jesus' name I ask it. Amen." Just one year later, servants came to check on their master's delay. They found him on his knees in prayer. He was dead.

Livingstone's testimony is powerful on many levels, but the one that is most striking is his claim upon Jesus as "my king." This has been a common declaration of the church throughout the ages. Even in our era, when democratic social movements topple kings and weigh in against tyrannical regimes, the largest social organization in the entire human race, the Church of Jesus Christ, holds as one of its core tenets of belief that Jesus is king.

Mary's beautiful song is one of the key passages undergirding all New Testament theological testimonies that declare Jesus to be king. Why should Jesus be a king? He was born into a poor family during a time of foreign occupation of their country. He was never trained in schools of leadership and had no desire to claim any throne. He seemed to alienate the rich and powerful, rebuffed the efforts of his disciples to start an armed rebellion, hushed the adulation of those who were the recipients of his mighty power, told the existing rulers that if he had a kingdom it was not in direct competition with theirs, and died an ignoble death meant for the worst of society's scalawags.

Yet from the first connections people made with Jesus, he was often identified as king. Foreigners traveled hundreds of miles to Judea when he was born, telling folks along the way of their astrological readings and projections: a truly great international king had been born! Palestine's powerful King Herod was afraid of Jesus and felt he might be competing for the throne Herod had worked so hard to control. Jesus' own words, while never clearly self-identifying him as a king, were constantly filled with language about the kingdom of heaven or the kingdom of God, of which he seemed to know a great deal more than anyone who was not directly connected with the key governing authority. Then, a Roman centurion assigned to Jesus' execution squad made the remarkable testimony, using language otherwise reserved only for the emperor himself, that "surely this man was the Son of God." Somehow people kept viewing Jesus as a king.

The affirmations only continued after Jesus disappeared from the scene. He is above all principalities and powers, Paul wrote, and said that every knee in heaven and on earth would bow to him. John saw him as an all-powerful ruler (Revelation 1) and had a vision of him as conquering king (v. 19). Even in their prayers, members of the early church addressed Jesus as "sovereign Lord," a term that could hardly be less than royal acknowledgement (Acts 5).

How did such nomenclature, which we today take for granted, come about? The key is in the promise made by God through Nathan to David in 2 Samuel 7. David was an unlikely king himself, set on a track to power during Israel's trial run at monarchy under the roller-coaster leadership of King Saul. Although he tried not to compete with the one he knew had also been selected for high office by Yahweh, David increasingly found himself on a trajectory that put him on Israel's throne. Yet he wanted, even there, to affirm that this nation's truest political structure was a theocracy.

The God of the Exodus and the Sinai Covenant was Israel's primary ruler.

For this reason, David brought the Ark of the Covenant, Yahweh's portable throne on earth, to Jerusalem, the new capital city of the nation (2 Samuel 6). Moreover, he wished for the building that would house the Ark to be a splendid palace, worthy of the nation's great king. To this task he set his purposes and resources, affirmed, at first, by his advisor, the prophet Nathan (v. 3).

Yet that night Nathan received a new word from the Lord. Although David's desires were laudable, he was too much a man of battle to build a palace of peace. David should gather the resources and make the plans, and then pass along to his son the mandate of temple-building.

But the prophetic word went further. Because David had tried to do the right thing, God wanted to honor him in a unique way. Although David was not permitted to build a house for God at this time, God would build a house for David. God made a pledge, a promise, a non-conditioned royal grant covenant to David. For all the years to come (as Randy Travis would sing: "Forever and ever. Amen!"), into perpetuity, David would have a descendent on the throne of the nation that was called God's chosen people.

This was an amazing commitment, and it came back in big ways as Israel's history unfolded. Even when Solomon's son Rehoboam should have lost the throne entirely, a remnant of the nation stuck with him as king. Their faithfulness to God's commitments proved accurate, for later the large portion of the nation that split off under Rehoboam's rival Jeroboam was destroyed by the Assyrian Empire in 722 BC. Through the shenanigans of Queen Athaliah and King Ahaz, or the turncoat despotism of King Manasseh, or the selfish panderings of Kings Jehoiakin and Zedekiah, Yahweh remained faithful to the divine promise, and the nation survived international threats that beat down many more powerful neighboring kingdoms. In fact, Judah was never really destroyed. While the Assyrians obliterated the Northern Kingdom, and Judah was made subject to Babylon for a while, a good portion of the nation survived intact as exiles. Eventually they returned to their patrimony and began hoping anew for the return of the Davidic monarchy and national restoration.

That's when good ancestral records became vitally important. Every family connected to the royal line would remember this promise of Yahweh and hope and pray that from their household the next great ruler would arise. So it was, that to an otherwise unimportant couple in Nazareth, about a thousand years after Yahweh made this pledge to David, a miraculous birth happened for two people who were both members of the royal family. On the basis of 2 Samuel 7, Jesus was born a king. While there was much that needed proof and confirmation about his character and his potential, once these things were seen by those around Jesus, the pieces quickly fell into place. That is why, when Jesus entered Jerusalem a week before his crucifixion, the crowds could shout with certainty and conviction, "Hosanna to the Son of David!" King Jesus had arrived.

For Israel, through the centuries of her sometimes much scarred existence, the promise of an eternal reign for David's great sons was like Christmas gifts bought early in November or December and packaged prettily for display under a tree until Christmas. One even has my name on it; all in the family know that it will bring me wonder, joy, and blessing, but its exact content remains a mystery until the wrappings are ripped away. So too with God's long-planned activity of salvation. The package was clearly set before the world in the national identity of Israel but until the specifics of the gift were revealed through the person of Jesus, it remained a "mystery." Even the prophets were somewhat in the dark about the exact contours of the great gift that was to be revealed. But now the wrappings are off, and the proclamation of Jesus is the hope of the world.

Some gifts we receive are simply add-ons to the polite niceties of the relationship. For instance, a man might give a woman a book as a Christmas gift. He knows she likes to read and this happens to be a best-seller she has not yet gotten into, so he gives it to her as a reflection of his thoughtfulness.

On a second level, however, other gifts might more directly tie into their relationship. He might buy a bottle of expensive perfume. When she opens the gift she is not only aware of his care but also enters a conspiracy with him toward a deepening level for their friendship. She applies the perfume to her body, and its scent becomes part of their special language of love. When she uses the perfume she thinks uniquely of him. When he smells the perfume, he thinks solely of her. The gift is not simply an add-on in their friendship; it has become a symbol of their relationship itself.

There is also a third level of gifting. Suppose the man and the woman are married. Along with gifts like books and perfumes they also have sexual intercourse as an expression of their love. When a baby is born, it is a gift for both of them, since neither could produce it alone. Yet it is more than just an outside gift that is brought into the relationship; it is itself the relationship come to expression. The gift is not just a thoughtful gesture (level 1) or even a meaningful enhancement to the relationship (level 2); this gift is the essence of the relationship come alive in a unique and special way (level 3).

So it is with Jesus. In the past God spoke of the divine commitment of care to the human race (providence; level 1). God also gave unique testimony of love through the nation of Israel (revelation; level 2). Now, however, God comes to live with us, to be part of our world and to transform our lives in ways that we had never before considered (salvation; level 3).

Mary is a marvelous figure. Although Reformers rightly reacted against the excesses of "Mariolatry," she deserves a lot more honor than many Protestants have accorded. So it would seem that today's gospel reading ought to raise Mary's name and identity as a key component in our Advent preaching. But that is not necessarily the case. Although the story is largely about Mary, the message is not. True, she is "highly favored," but when Gabriel explains why, the focus is on Jesus, not Mary. She will conceive and bear a son, but the son's name is already declared (mother Mary has no choice in the matter). Her son (not her) will be great. In fact, he will be identified with God, not Mary. And all the promises made to great King David in 2 Samuel 7 will come true in this person she will carry for nine months.

Even when Mary questions how such marvelous tales could become reality, she is again set in the background. "The Holy Spirit will come upon you, and the power of the most high will overshadow you." Mary will be acted upon and almost consumed under the weight of glory that crushes her. The only thing people will remark about, as these things unfold, is that "the holy one to be born will be called the Son of God."

Why does Luke tell us the story this way? He reminds us, at the beginning (Luke 1:1-4), that there are other reflections on the life and teachings of Jesus in circulation. Mark, in his gospel, did not think it appropriate even to talk about the weakness of Jesus when he was just a baby; so his tale begins as the full-grown Jesus strides decisively through the hills and valleys of Galilee, healing and teaching and proclaiming the kingdom of God in sanctified frenzy. Later in the century John, too, will follow this path, speaking of Jesus' initial coming only in the metaphors of philosophy and liturgical symbolism. And Matthew's approach included a few notes about Jesus' miraculous birth but tied them quickly to stories of other great deliverers who were born to save Israel.

Luke's purpose is more clearly seen when the gospel as a whole is read with care. Among the many things that mark Luke's literary passions and style is his desire to locate the story and message of Jesus within its historical context. These are the days of Caesar Augustus, and Quirinius, and Pontius Pilate, and Claudius. The way that Luke relates the events and actions of Jesus' life reflect on incidents that others in the larger Greco-Roman world would appreciate quickly. Everyone knew, for example, that Cyrus the Great of the Persians, who had conquered the Babylonians and sent the Jewish exiles home, was miraculously born. His mother claimed that on the night of his conception a bolt of lightning had flamed from heaven and pierced her womb. That is why her son became powerful, a ruler of nations.

So too with the next "great" ruler of recent history. Alexander, born to Philip of Macedon (supposedly a direct descendent of the god Heracles) and his wife Olympias, was reputed to have come along only when one of the gods visited each of them in dreams and declared the divine qualities of their future son. Not only that, but the Temple of Artemis (or Dianna) in Ephesus caught fire the night Alexander was born. Rumor had it that the gods were so busy midwifing this birth that they neglected their usual care of that honored site.

Then there was the case of Caesar Augustus himself. An astrologer had foretold incredible things about him when he was born. Although his early years as Gaius Octavius Jr., did not betray great promise, by the time he was twelve he gave a funeral oration for his grandmother that stunned the crowds with its insight, passion, and brilliance. He was on his way to become a divinely appointed ruler.

While Luke would not wish to merely place Jesus among that crowd as a product of myth and superstition, he does understand that the exceptionally great leaders among the nations are prepared and equipped by God. Thus, at the start of Jesus' life story, it is important to Luke that the great divine plans be highlighted. Only in this way will the full impact of Jesus' ministry be understood.

So we need to honor Mary. But we must be careful not to take any of the attention from her son. Mary's role in the birth of the Messiah was truly unique. Yet it was only a portion of the long and heaven-directed planning by which God took up residence on earth for the salvation of all nations. This is Luke's emphasis and Mary's song. The balances of power on earth are about to be tipped through this new king, born in the most unlikely of circumstances.

So how do we measure power? Alan Redpath tells of a prominent businessman in South Africa who was duly impressed with the luxury of Rolls Royce automobiles. He ordered one for himself and marveled at its speed and handling. He looked through the manual but found no test results listed indicating the horsepower of the engine. So he went to the dealer.

"I'm sorry," the dealer told him. "The company never states the horsepower of their engines."

But the man was not to be put off and he was too powerful a person to be ignored. So the dealer sent a cable to Derby, England, asking the head office for an answer in the matter.

Within a short time, there was a reply. It was brief and to the point, a response of only a single word. How much horsepower does the Rolls Royce engine develop? "Adequate." That's all. That's enough.

So it is in the birth story of Jesus. The power of God will come down and engender this powerful life. How powerful will the baby be? He will be king. With how much authority? Enough. Adequate. To rule all nations on earth and everything within them will change. Amen.

**Christmas Eve / Day**
**Luke 2:1-14 (15-20)**

# *The Wrong Gift*

What did you get for Christmas?

We shouldn't ask it, but we do, don't we? It is part and parcel of our experience of the season. While Christmas gift-giving may have originated in Christian communities seeking to celebrate the divine gift to us, it is now our culture that demands we spend and purchase and drive the economy into the black through our holiday purchases.

We are obligated to give gifts. We are cajoled into giving. We must find the "right" gift for each person on our list. Can you do it? Did you do it? Is this the year you got it right?

Tomorrow says, "No." Tomorrow half of those who received gifts will go back to the stores to return them and exchange them or get refunds so that they can buy what they really wanted. Yesterday we bought the perfect gifts. Tomorrow they will all be wrong.

But we are in good company. God got it wrong, too, that first Christmas. That's essentially what we read at first glance in Luke's report. We are so familiar with the words that we often skim past the meaning. If we put Jesus' birth back into its historical context, God gave the wrong gift to the wrong people wrapped in the wrong package!

Here's how. First, note how Luke ties the events of Jesus' life directly to circumstances in the greater Roman world. He reports that Jesus' birth occurred during the reign of Caesar Augustus and the governorship of Quirinius (Luke 2:1-2), and later tells that the beginnings of Jesus' ministry took place in the fifteenth year of Tiberius Caesar's rule (Luke 3:1). The connection with Caesar Augustus is particularly striking, since Augustus was the great ruler who brought about the *Pax Romana*, the peace of Rome. For the past fourteen years the doors of the temple of the god Janus in Rome had been closed. During the decades prior to that they had stood open, as they always did when there were battles afoot, and the Legions were in the fields to the north and the east. But Caesar Augustus had brilliantly subdued the world and peace was his great gift to the expansive empire that embraced all.

So no new peace was needed. In fact, no one was looking for a new ruler. Caesar was "god" and the world rejoiced in his benevolence.

And yet... and yet there had to be the nagging fear at the edge of the collective social conscience that even Caesar's marvelous peace could never last. Sin has made us for war, and we have lived out that symptom in bloody colors at every turn.

Now the angels sing that God is bringing "peace" to earth through this gift of Jesus on Christmas morning. It doesn't make sense in the middle of the *Pax Romana*. It shouldn't make sense. But it does. For in a very few years the great Roman Empire would begin to fray and disintegrate, and only the kingdom of Jesus would survive its collapse. It seemed, on every hand, like the wrong gift. Only time would tell a different story.

God's gift was not only the wrong gift, according to the times, but it was also given to the wrong people. Luke makes evident, particularly through the song of the angels to the shepherds that even in those times of relative calm, the greater gift of divine peace was needed by humankind and could be brought only through Jesus.

Who were these shepherds? We think of boys in their dads' bathrobes play-acting in Christmas pageants. And through nostalgic eyes we see little boy David on the hillsides of ancient Judah. By the days of Jesus' birth, shepherds had become the outsiders of society. They were considered ritually impure, socially inept, thieves and robbers, and perpetual liars. They were not allowed in synagogues or the great temple in Jerusalem. Bouncers at the doors turned back any who might get a conscience and think he should pray. Rabbis railed against them, forbidding people ever to do business with them, let alone enter their despised trade. Because shepherds paid no attention to property lines when herding their flocks, they spoiled backyards and swiped things that were not locked down. No shepherd was allowed to testify in court, for it was widely known that they were all liars and couldn't tell a truth if it whacked them in the face.

So if God is going to do something nice for the human race, the least he could do is bring a gift to people who deserved it. Yet here the familiar nativity story takes us where we truly do not want to be. When we find out about the shepherds, we stay away from them, like the lost and the last and the least in all our societies. How could God do such a thing? First God gives a gift we don't need, and then God sends it to the wrong address, as if these losers know what to do with it! How odd of God!

But the wrongness doesn't end there. The wrong gift to the wrong people is wrapped up in the wrong package. As George MacDonald put it in one of his fine and perceptive poems:

> *They all were looking for a king*
> *To slay their foes and lift them high;*
> *Thou cam'st a little Baby thing*
> *That made a mother cry.*
>       — "They All Were Looking for a King"
>       George MacDonald, 1883 (public domain)

If we get a gift from God, certainly it ought to be something we can use. We need power. We need wealth. We need healing. We need recognition. We need things.

All we get is a baby! A helpless baby! It doesn't make sense!

That's where we need to take another look at what is going on here. Although the gospels of the New Testament are among the most widely recognized and read literary documents in the world, it remains difficult to explain their exact genre. They have no parallel in any other religious or literary tradition.

Certainly the gospels are not mere biographies. They do not offer enough data about the life of Jesus to construct a full story of his existence or to offer a well-developed social portrait of his presence among his contemporaries.

Nor is it true that the gospels are a complete and systematic summary of Jesus' teachings. What has been preserved as the record of Jesus' sayings and speeches is too haphazardly gathered to form a codified compendium that would neatly explain his wisdom or theology.

The most fitting designation for the gospels seems to be "proclamation." These documents are records of early Christian preaching about Jesus, describing the significance of his coming, the meaning of his person, the content of his teachings, the impact of his actions, the character of his death, and the miracle of his resurrection. This is exactly what Luke tells us at the start of his gospel.

Jesus is the center of history, according to the Bible. The very term "gospel" means "good news." In a world that is plagued with bad news, Jesus' coming and presence reminds us that God wants to love us, care about us, and help us understand the ethics and morality of the kingdom of God that protects and affirms us. That's why the preaching of the church is always about Jesus. And it begins with the gospels.

Luke starts his gospel with a quick personal note to Theophilus, who is a friend and recent convert to Christianity.

Theophilus may have been a highly placed government leader, since Luke calls him "most excellent." More interesting, though, is the man's name. "Theophilus" means "friend of God." Whether this was the name given to him by his parents or a nickname he claimed when he became a Christian, it is a marvelous title for all who read about Jesus and call him Savior and Lord.

As Luke notes, becoming a Christian is always a kind of homecoming. The gift of God announced to the shepherds is designed to bring them home. "For to you is born today, in the city of David..." We are all displaced people, whether in little or great ways. The gospel story reminds us that God came into our world in the person of Jesus to find us and to bring us home to love and grace and eternity itself.

When we actually begin to breathe the air of the gospels, they smell of home. Christopher Fry put it this way in one of his plays, *The Lady's not for Burning*: Margaret and Nicholas are talking about a woman who seems to be acting strangely. Margaret says, "She must be lost." Nicholas responds, wistfully, "Who isn't? The best thing we can do is to make whatever we're lost in look as much like home as we can."

That's what we do with our lives, isn't it? We have so many goals and dreams and hopes in life, yet so few of them pan out. We get old before we've done half of what we wanted. Somehow we never become what we thought we might. We make a few mistakes along the way. We disappoint some people, and they disappoint us. Even our best times have an edge of bitterness attached to them — when they end we walk away nursing our nostalgia. We're always a little bit away from home — from the home we remember or the home we desire; from the dream we miss or the dream we're still looking for. That's what Nicholas is saying to Margaret in Christopher Fry's play. We're all a bit lost in life. We're all a bit away from home. The best we can do is make what we have look as much as possible like what we think "home" should be, until we can finally see our true home, and like Luke, bring our friends along with us.

No matter where we go, no matter what we do, there must live in each of us a touch of that homesickness, or we die a horrible death. Our trips "home" are only a pale imitation of the place we belong and merely a wayside rest stop on a restless journey to the real home of God's love and God's eternity. More than we know that is where we all truly want to go. Only in finding Jesus and the coming of God's kingdom will our desires find fulfillment and our longings be satisfied. Only then will our homesickness end.

That is why this "wrong" gift of God keeps giving each year. Perhaps it is not the gift that is "wrong," but we, the ones who beg and borrow and steal, really don't know what we need. I'm sure that was the case for Mary and Joseph as they wrestled with these things, "pondering them," as Luke puts it.

Think of it! Whenever a new president is elected, tabloids and journals bump sales by profiling the arrival of the next "First Family." Women's clothing choices, children's behavior, couple's tenderness or standoffishness, are duly chronicled. Some First Families create idyllic portraits of the closest thing Americans will have to royalty (the Kennedys and "Camelot"). Others bring homespun commonness into the White House (the Carters). A few depict dynasties in the making (the Bushes, first and second), while others seem to leap off the silver screen and bring Hollywood to life (the Reagans). A few seem to be political teams (the Clintons, the Obamas), although one always defers publicly to the other as a matter of domestic efficiency and diplomatic focus.

Perhaps it is because our lives are eternally caught up in the drama of naming, claiming, and defaming cultural icons that some families stand above us as types and symbols of greater meaning and significance. It happens in the church too. We are more than a little curious about the First Family of Christianity. We pick up prescient clues from the Old Testament prophecies that we recite about Jesus and theology as romantic drama, looking for more details about wedding dresses and royal ceremonies. When the marriage is consummated, we are the first on hand with Luke to view the special days of celebration in the life of the First Family of which everyone is talking.

When children play "dress up" they are enacting common social rituals. Lovers dress up for special dates. Spouses dress up to go out for an evening. Actors dress up to get on stage. Soldiers dress up for the parade march. Business leaders dress up for the big meeting. Children dress up for the first day of school. Gangs dress up in the right colors for identity. Football fans dress up in team pigments. Choirs dress up for performance. To dress up is to enter a community of kindred spirits or to take up a role of identity.

On this first day of a new Christmas season, in which we bow to the God who keeps promises and enters our world, we enjoy the music of caroling, keeping alive the attention of our world to the big news — the good news — the dawning of a new age in which Camelot begins all over again, and this time will not have within her secret places the specter of her own destruction. For the bridegroom who adorns his bride has already found and dealt with the skeletons in every closet.

On this first day of a New Age, the weeping and wailing of another frightful swing around the sun is like the distant voices on the last amusement park ride, and the song of the dawn is hope and joy and expectation. You can see it glowing on the faces of those in the First Family!

Our culture seems gossip hungry and celebrity frenzied. Popular actors are identified as "stars," and people's lives are scrutinized by tabloids simply because they have wealth or public notoriety.

Sometimes in the church, especially in the Protestant tradition, the lives and times of the First Family of faith are underplayed. Religion becomes overly spiritual and the incredible reality of God entering the realities of daily lives to create humble human superstars through whom history is changed forever can be lost. Today is a great day to play up the significance of our First Family of faith, and how we have been re-energized by knowing they are there. Let the radiance of heaven diffuse a new "Camelot" glow through the admiration God and we can give to this First Family, in which the drama of divine romance with us takes on human form.

There is an interesting, albeit limited, parallel to draw between Caesar Augustus, the mighty Roman emperor who brooded over the world at the time of Jesus' birth, and Christ himself. All who saw what Caesar looked like never expected him to gain exalted position in society. Here is how those who knew him described him: He is quite short; he has such sensitive skin that he dares not be out in the sun too long — and never without his head covered; he walks with a limp; his right hand fails him from time to time, so he rarely uses it; bladder stones cause him daily pain; he doesn't sleep well; he catches cold easily; and horseback riding tires him, so he is often carried to the battlefield on a litter.

Can you imagine a man bearing that description becoming the great Caesar Augustus? Yet he did. Part of his secret lies in an event that occurred when he was a young boy. One day he visited the well-known astrologer and fortune-teller Theogenes. When Theogenes read the boy's horoscope, he was so impressed with its prophecy that he fell on his face and worshiped him.

You and I may not believe in astrology, but Cesar Augustus did. All throughout the struggles of his life, he lived as if this prophecy were true, and eventually it became true.

How much more significant is this prophecy for Christ and for us? Jesus certainly knew the meaning that God's long history of salvation placed squarely on his shoulders. But those of us who become the ongoing incarnation of Christ in this world share his identity as well and need ever and again to become what we are meant to be: the servant of God for the redemptive transformation of God's world.

The wrong gift? For the wrong people? In the wrong packaging?

Perhaps not! Amen.

**Christmas 1**
**Luke 2:41-52**

# *In Praise of Praise*

Our English word "carol" emerged from the public celebrations of late medieval France. It was originally a term used to describe joyful singers circling a flute player. While the subject of the ballads in those early years of "caroling" could be anything that brought a smile to the face and a lilt to the heart and a jig to the step, the word was quickly tied to the singers of Christmas and their songs in praise of God who did wondrous things in the incarnation of Jesus.

So it is that the music of Christmas is now always "caroled." Caroling is the singing of wonder, praise, and joy. One of the great preachers of the past said that when we speak of ordinary things, any old face would do, but when telling the story of salvation, only a radiant smile could communicate the message.

A woman remembered going with her father to a hospital on a Christmas morning as he conducted worship for those who were isolated from families and friends. She recalled her father's passion about the birth stories of Jesus, and the wonder that filled his eyes when he exclaimed the great power and mystery of God's love. When the little congregation sang Christmas carols with feeble voices and warbling weariness, the preacher increased his own passionate praise until all were energized in a holy glow.

All, that is, except one of the charge nurses who was not too happy to be stuck with this Christmas shift and its bothersome holiday extras. She played the part of Nurse Ratched in stellar type-casting. No quiver of a smile had a chance on her grim lips, no flicker of faith would ever sparkle in her eyes.

The young girl carried some of her father's preacherly boldness in her heart, and when the service was over, stood in front of the prim sourpuss demanding, "Aren't you a Christian?"

However inappropriate the challenge from a child who should be seen and not heard, the nurse responded with professional dignity: "Of course I am."

"Then," said the budding evangelist, "your heart should tell your face!"

So it should be with us, on this first Sunday of Christmas. It is indeed a time for caroling, for singing, for dancing, for contagious chorusing. Robert Rainy, Principal of New College in Edinburgh late in the nineteenth century, described joy as "the flag which flies over the castle when the king is in residence." How apt! Joy flutters and catches the breeze. Joy animates the colors of its components. Joy tells the story of the one who resides in the big house. Joy is the song of delight that echoes in the stirring renditions of national anthems when peace, hope, and expectation are the hues of the day.

Rainy used the analogy to explain to his niece what it meant for Jesus to bring joy. God come home. God near at hand. God making the world right. God taking up residence among us. This is the message of Christmas, and the echo of our texts for today. God has returned to the castle of earth's kingdoms, the rightful Lord and master, and those who know it sing with joy.

This, of course, is why young Jesus' appearance in the temple creates an ironic moment for those who think they know the place. They have been left a castle and have supposed, for too long, that the king was gone. With an absentee landlord, others had taken over, and tried to redecorate it to their tastes. They installed wall hangings matching their own perspectives on beauty and decorum and filled the library shelves with echoes of their own wisdom.

Suddenly, however, a young boy turns up who seems to know the king better than they remembered him. The lad whispers wisdom that sounds like the prophets who spoke on the king's behalf. And the youngster even talks in familiar terms about seeing the king face-to-face. How can this be? What does it mean?

L. Nelson Bell, the father-in-law of Billy Graham, was a medical missionary in China for much of his career. One of the earliest converts to Christianity under his ministry was a wizened old man who later church members simply called "Elder Cao." When Dr. Bell asked Elder Cao to tell some visitors why he had become a Christian, the elderly gentleman put it simply.

"A man fell into a deep and slimy pit," said Elder Cao, "and he was unable to get out. Along came the Buddha. He stopped and took pity on the man. 'If you will come up here to me,' said the Buddha, 'I will teach you the way of enlightenment and you will never fall into the pit again.' But the man could not get out of the pit, so the Buddha went on to bring enlightenment to others.

"Along came Confucius, and he too was moved with compassion by the plight of the man in the pit. 'If you will listen to my teachings,' said Confucius, 'you will understand how society is formed, and what can be done to prevent anyone from falling into the pit.' Then he, too, went on, for the man did not rise out of the pit.

"Finally," said Elder Cao, "Jesus came along. As with the others, he was filled with concern for the man in the pit. So he jumped down into the pit and helped the man get out.

"This," said Elder Cao, "is why I am a Christian."

This is what people experienced that day when Jesus came to the temple, even though he was only twelve. They recognized the depth of his wisdom but more than that, they felt, through him, that the king had returned to the castle and joy was the only true response. Amen.

**New Year's Day**
**Matthew 25:31-46**

# *At the Gate of the Year*

Time is the news of the day. Yesterday was yesteryear. Today we wipe the slates clean, turn the ledger page to a new fiscal period, and leaf through the engaging photos that will mark the progress of the calendar we freshly hang. Time is on our minds, even if it is only a hangover from last night's partying. What time is it?

Einstein got it right, of course: time is relative. We're all related to it! And it treats us differently as we hold its hand. Says the poet:

*When as a child I laughed and wept, Time crept.*
*When as a youth I waxed more bold, Time strolled.*
*When I became a full-grown man, Time ran.*
*When older still I daily grew, Time flew.*
*Soon I shall find, in passing on, Time gone.*
   — *Time Paces*, Henry Twells, 1823-1900 (public domain)

Why does time seem to speed up as we age? Roy Drusky, in a classic song of decades ago, crooned about the variable speeds of time like this:

*I've been up and I've been down I've worked the fields I've plowed the ground*
*I've taken strain and pressure till I thought I might explode*
*Now I yearn for childhood days of model planes and lemonade*
*When the day stretched out before me like a long long Texas road*
*Yes a long long Texas road bout a million miles or so*
*When you're just a child there ain't no time but now*

> *Must have left that long old road seven hundred years ago*
> *And I'd find it once again if I knew how*

Drusky contemplates the rush and frenzy of his life, wishing, at least for a morning, to rejoin his younger self in the careless play of a lazy Texas day. But he also knows that nostalgia is yesterday's prices at today's wages and an unreal world that can never be found. It is the true "Neverland" of Peter Pan and what is given up to reach it costs more dearly than the price is worth. So Drusky continues his musings:

> *So I watch the children play and dream my dreams of yesterday*
> *Don't tell them to be grateful I'm sure that they've been told*
> *If I knew then what I know now that would have messed it up somehow*
> *When the day stretched out before me like a long long Texas road*
>     — "Long Long Texas Road," Roy Drusky (public domain)

Entering a new year is a moment in which time and its relativity becomes very meaningful. A year ago there were folks in our congregation who are no longer with us. Others of us will not survive this calendar year. So the question of the day is how will we turn the ticking of the clock into moments of meaning while we can. Welcome to the new year of our Lord!

Jesus pits tick-tock time against meaningful moments in this famous passage. In essence, he challenges us in a comparison between *chronos* and *kairos*, between the chronology of events that happen in succession and the significance they build as an era that we can define. It is an important gem tucked into a dark caldron of despair. We think we are doing this and that and the next thing, bopping along in time, and suddenly the eyes of eternity are on us and the meaning of everything changes.

When I was in high school, a revival swept our area, and many of us pondered big questions of life and meaning together. A friend and I formed a Bible study group that was actually more of a social club in which we tried to wrestle with faith and angst while sheltered in the home of some trusted adults who were not yet over the horrible age of thirty. We would meet together on Sunday evenings, often deciding only when we arrived what we were going to "study" that night. Invariably, Jeff, hidden back in a corner between sofas and stuffed chairs, would murmur that we should read Ecclesiastes because he was depressed and it was depressing and maybe these two woeful laments would find each other and somehow make the world right.

Jeff was onto something, of course. Ecclesiastes is indeed a rather dark and depressing diatribe. "All is meaningless!" is the cry, both in the beginning (Ecclesiastes 1:2) and again at the end (Ecclesiastes 12:8). In between there are lists after lists of things that only prove the teacher's dark and troubling point of view:

- A king builds a massive empire and his successor wastes it to nothing (2:12).
- A man wrestles out an education that makes him incredibly perceptive, but he dies the same death as a fool and is forgotten (2:13-14).
- A man works all his life to create a marvelous and productive estate, but there is no one to leave it to and he dies alone (4:7-8).
- A wealthy man amasses greater fortunes but dies consumed by greed (5:10-12).

The litany is incessant and drums its way into our brains like a leaky faucet chasing away sleep on a muggy and worrisome night. Wisdom, pleasure, folly, toil — they all come to nothing (1:12—2:26). Time itself is a cruel taskmaster that binds and breaks down (v. 3). Other dimensions of life leave us hopeless: oppression, hard work, friendlessness, political advancement, unfulfilled vows to God, amassing wealth (4:1—6:12).

My friend Jeff was right. Ecclesiastes is depressing. But that is only the beginning of the story. On its surface, and especially at its beginning, the screaming message is this: *All we do and everything that happens to us is ultimately meaningless and has no lasting value!* But if we take the time to hear the notes of hopeful optimism that begin to leak through, starting here in chapter 3, a more moderate message speaks out: *Yet life goes on, so let's make the best of it and be more wise about it than foolish.* And if we attune our ears to the religious confidence that forms a bedrock foundation underlying all of the teacher's reflections, a subtle but profound message whispers as well: *Life can only mean something if there is a God who sets the values (e.g., time and morality) and gives us a link to eternity that confirms our right to exist.*

This is the meaning of Jesus' parable for us. While we get caught up in time, doing little things that in and of themselves may or may not have existence, God monitors the whole of our existence and stamps it all with meaning. But, of course, we have to be doing things that align with the values of heaven.

The ancient Greeks talked of death as the passage across the River Styx into the region of the underworld where shades and shadows of departed persons rested uneasily in Hades. The River Styx was the domain of Charon, the ferryman of death. His job was to bring newcomers across the river to their final abode. Before they stepped into his boat, however, Charon always reminded his passengers that they could avail themselves of the opportunity to drink from the waters of Lethe. These magical springs had the power to make one forget, a transaction that carries with it both blessings and curses, as the movie *Eternal Sunshine of the Spotless Mind* portrayed.

One woman who came to Charon seemed eager to make use of Lethe's powers, according to a Greek legend. "I will forget how I suffered," she said quickly. "Remember that you will also forget how you have rejoiced," Charon added quietly. "Yes," she replied, "but I will forget my failures." "So too your victories," came the rejoinder. "Oh, but I will forget how I have been hated," the woman went on. "True," opined the ferryman, "and also how you have been loved."

The legend tells of how this final word caused her to pause and shortly after step into Charon's craft without tasting the waters of Lethe. Sometimes starting over requires as much that we remember as that we forget.

This is certainly true in the Christian gospel. John's vision of a new heaven and a new earth in Revelation 21 does not wipe the slate clean entirely as the do-over begins. Instead, there is a purging process that brings with it memories of the greatest acts of God and humankind, while sanitizing out those bits that the devil spit in with tarnish. We recognize all the elements of this scene: Heaven is there, as it has hovered over our world from the beginning. Earth remains, though chastened and restored. Then comes Jerusalem, David's city, the temple town, and symbol of how closely humans can reach toward heaven while the Creator stoops down to touch their fingers. Then a throne appears, not unlike the combination of the Ark of the Covenant, Yahweh's portable dais during Israel's wanderings, and the grand seat of messianic royalty established by the royal grant of 2 Samuel 7.

The same old, same old is wonderfully new as the tears are gone, the frustrations dissipate, the scything specter of death has disappeared, and pain is no longer needed as a divine megaphone (á la Paul Brand and Philip Yancey) calls us wandering wretches home.

What a scene for a new year's morning! It's the kind of thing singer Murray McLaughlin penned for a year-end holiday song in 1989:

*May I get what I want, not what I deserve*
*May the coming year not throw a single curve*
*May I hurt nobody, may I tell no lies*
*If I can't go on, give me strength to try*
*Ring the old year out, Ring the new year in*
*Bring us all good luck, Let the good guys win*

*May the one you like be the one you get*
*May you get some place you haven't been to yet*
*May your friends surround you, never do you wrong*
*May your eyes be clear, may your heart be strong*
*Ring the old year out, Ring the new year in*
*Bring us all good luck, Let the good guys win*
— "Let the Good Guys Win"
Murray McLaughlin (public domain)

Of course, McLaughlin's prayer and hope is John's testimony and anticipated reality. Whatever the new year brings, today is a day of confidence for the child of God. It is indeed "The Year of Our Lord," and we know how the story ends. Or perhaps, finally truly begins.

No doubt a few New Year's resolutions have already been made and broken. Jonathan Edwards' string of commitments, to be "read over... once a week," is a rather demanding exercise in spiritual sanitization:

- Resolved, that I will do whatsoever I think to be most to the glory of God, and my own good, profit, and pleasure, in the whole of my duration; without any consideration of the time, whether now, or never so many myriads of ages hence.
- Resolved, to do whatever I think to be my duty and most for the good and advantage of humankind in general.
- Resolved, never to lose one moment of time, but to improve it in the most profitable way I possibly can.
- Resolved, to live with all my might, while I do live.
- Resolved, never to do anything, which I would be afraid to do if it were the last hour of my life.
- Resolved, never to do anything out of revenge.
- Resolved, never to speak evil of anyone, so that it shall tend to his dishonor, more or less, upon no account except for some real good.

- Resolved, to study the scriptures so steadily, constantly, and frequently, as that I may find, and plainly perceive, myself to grow in the knowledge of the same.
- Resolved, never to count that a prayer, nor to let that pass as a prayer, nor that as a petition of prayer, which is so made, that I cannot hope that God will answer it; nor that as a confession which I cannot hope God will accept.
- Resolved, to ask myself, at the end of every day, week, month, and year, wherein I could possibly, in any respect have done better.
- Resolved, never to give over, nor in the least to slacken, my fight with my corruption, however unsuccessful I may be.
- Resolved, after afflictions, to inquire, what I am the better for them; what good I have got by them; and what I might have got by them.
- Resolved, always to do that, which I shall wish I had done when I see others do it.

These are certainly commendable promises. The outcome of a life lived as Jonathan Edwards so pledged would probably look a lot like that envisioned by Jesus in today's gospel reading. But there is a subtle difference. Notice that the actions Jesus commends are all good and upright, moral and socially transforming. But notice as well that those who do such things, to the glory of God and the honor of Jesus, don't even realize what they are doing. It is not a checklist of perfections that they mark with a pious pen. Instead, it is a lifestyle of other-focus that leads to blessings on those around them.

New Year's resolutions are appropriate, to a degree, since self-discipline is one of the most powerful educational devices available to the human race. Moreover, goals are extremely important in building a life of significance, for "he who aims at nothing will always be certain to achieve it!" But spirituality is never served best when packaged in its nutritional information and festooned with a snobbish price tag that boldly declares, "See what a good boy am I!"

Instead, the point of Jesus' teaching is to tumble our New Year's resolutions on end and develop eyes for the world around us. If, by the close of this new year, the edges of darkness are pushed back slightly, children have slept in greater peace, sores have been soothed, and loneliness reduced, then Jesus' parable will have taken root, and we won't even have noticed it. But others will!

In the words of Murray McLaughlin:

*May the times to come be the best you've had*
*May peace rule the world and let it make us glad*
*When you see something wrong, try to make it right*
*Put a shadowed world into the bright sunlight*
*Ring the old year out, Ring the new year in*
*Bring us all good luck, Let the good guys win*
— "Let the Good Guys Win"
Murray McLaughlin (public domain)

*Chronos* happens to us, and we fill it with minutiae — the daily reports in journals, news, and business quarterlies. But *kairos* is what Billy Graham always called "the hour of decision," and what T.S. Eliot pointed to as "the moment that gives meaning." How will this "Year of Our Lord" reach upward from *chronos* to *kairos*? What will lift the ticking of the clock into an eternal destiny of significance?

Minnie Louise Harkins (1875-1957) penned a poignant reflection that serves well each New Year's celebration:

*I said to the man who stood at the gate of the year*
*"Give me a light that I may tread safely into the unknown."*
*And he replied,*
*"Go into the darkness and put your hand into the hand of God*
*That shall be to you better than light and safer than a known way!"*
— *At the Gate of the Year* (public domain)

New Year's Day makes us think about time and opportunity. In that context, Robert H. Smith summarized well what we all know:

*The clock of life is wound but once,*
*And no man has the power*
*To tell just when the hands will stop*
*At late or early hour.*
— *The Clock of Life* (public domain)

We are bound by time, the great organizer of all that we experience. We cannot return to yesterday except in our memories, and these do not allow us to change anything that has already taken place. Human (and, for that matter, universal) existence is hung on the sweeping hands of time. We do not understand time. We cannot control time. Even when we explore the relativity of our experiences of time we are unable to alter its massive grip and pull on our existence.

One of the most fascinating stories of human history is told by William Manchester in his masterful *A World Lit Only by Fire*. In it he describes medieval Europe and the communities during the time that were entirely regulated by the cycles of the sun. Time had a much more immediate grip on life, for virtually nothing happened in society that was not directly linked to the presence or absence of the sun, and even its angle above the horizon. We have pushed back the night with our artificial lighting and challenged the tyranny of the aging process with our chemicals and plastic surgeries that pretend to be a magician's wand cure for the malady of time's inevitable march across our bodies. Still, everyone who is born, dies. Every plant, even the mightiest oak, topples. Every age goes to war, vowing this will be the one to end it all. Every masterful Roman forum becomes, eventually, a tourist trap ringed by cappuccino cafes. No tears can last forever, nor will the straightjacket of sorrow win forever against happiness. Time wrestles all into its incessant, rhythmic beat.

But why? Why did God invent time as a prerequisite for life on planet earth? Could we not bop about through space staying forever young? The writer of Ecclesiastes is sober enough to know that such speculations lead nowhere. But he also has begun to show grudging appreciation for time as life's great organizing principle. Time makes sure that we all move in the same direction at the same rate. Time provides the context for memory and hope. Time destabilizes pain, even while it takes the edge off excessive hilarity. Time is the janitor that keeps the classes moving through the school so that they don't get stuck in "Hotel California."

Then comes Jesus' affirmation. We live in time, but eternity tells us why. It is like Grant Tuller's marvelous reflection:

*My life is but a weaving*
*Between my Lord and me,*
*I cannot choose the colors*
*He worketh steadily.*

*Oftimes He weaveth sorrow,*
*And I in foolish pride*
*Forget He sees the upper*
*And I, the under side.*

*Not till the loom is silent*
*And the shuttles cease to fly*
*Shall God unroll the canvas*
*And explain the reason why.*

*The dark threads are as needful*
*In the Weaver's skillful hand*
*As the threads of gold and silver*
*In the pattern He has planned.*
— *The Weaver* (public domain)

Amen.

**Epiphany of Our Lord**
**Matthew 2:1-12**

# *Shine, Jesus, Shine!*

In their book *Resident Aliens*, Stanley Hauerwas and William Willimon tell the story of a United Methodist congregation whose education committee was determined to make Confirmation a meaningful exercise. They held discussions as to the preferred outcomes and then drew up a master plan by which the high school seniors would be partnered with more mature members of the congregation in order to be mentored into adult Christian responsibilities.

Young Max was teamed with 24-year-old Joe, a single fellow who seemed to have his head on straight and worked well with young people. Several weeks into the venture, however, Joe called the pastor in great distress. He wanted someone to put Max in his place and make him behave. Gently the pastor tried to soothe Joe's obviously frayed nerves and calm him to a place where talk could regain its balance.

Slowly the problem emerged. Joe was fine with meeting Max now and again and telling him some stuff about the Christian faith. He had even dropped the remark that Max could come by sometime, if he wanted, and the two of them could hang out together. Well, it seems as if Max thought Joe meant it, for he came by Joe's house unannounced, in what turned out to be a very awkward moment. Joe had been in bed with his girlfriend, and there was no easy way to cover it up. Joe was embarrassed, and turned it all on Max, blaming him for intruding on Joe's personal life. Max, in turn, delivered a blistering accusation against Joe for being a phony and said that if it was all right for Joe to have sex with his girlfriend, Max could do the same. Now Joe was caught in a host of moral lies and inconsistencies and the shouting match ended with Joe telling Max to get out. Max stomped off and slammed the door, and Joe called the pastor in irritation over the whole mess.

What had begun as a venture in modeling Christian behavior to those entering adult religious responsibilities had turned into an object lesson in the moral quagmire of general church life. M. Scott Peck wrote that one of the most unlikely places to create true community in modern North American society is in the church, because we have bought into isolation and performance mentalities. Joe and Max only proved the truth of this, and they were but a symptom of a much larger problem in most of our congregations. We gather on Sundays to say pious things about God and morality, but we live isolated and hidden lives in which we too often don't practice what we preach. When we get caught in our lies and deceptions, as in the case of Max and Joe, we attack each other or we complain that the system is broken.

Epiphany Sunday reminds us that the secret things will be brought to light. God shines a powerful beam into our world in the person of Jesus Christ. All who come into this radiance begin to glow or hide, depending on their lifestyle. As Matthew reminds us, some delight in the light of eternity, while others seek to snuff it out. Epiphany, the revealing of God into our world, is a moment of crisis.

Aren't we always on the edge of crisis? A spate of apocalyptic movies has toured the silver screens of our world recently. A jilted planet fights back in *The Happening* and nearly destroys the human race in a bid for ecological survival. *War of the Worlds* has fetid aliens drugging it up on human blood until they catch a nasty virus from our biological systems and die ignobly as their harvesting spacecraft slam into skyscrapers and their crews melt down into sticky ooze. In *Star Trek*, time-traveling Romulans seek to annihilate the worlds (including earth) that produced their enemies before those combatants had a chance to be born. An earlier episode in the series had the *Enterprise* taking "The Voyage Home" in order to prevent earth's destruction by its ancient alien creators, siblings of our oceans' whales, who no longer heard the cry of the humpbacks from their outer space listening posts. More recently on *The Day the Earth Stood Still*, interstellar civilizations have determined that humans are destroying earth, one of the few planets rich enough in resources to serve as home to multiple varieties of organic life, and so a ship of destruction is dispatched, only to be thwarted in its endeavors when its robotic captain, while assuming human form in order to communicate, begins to understand homo sapiens' complexities and calls off the destruction. Even shows aimed at children get in on the act with the *Transformers* vividly portraying the battle between human-hating Decepticons and human-loving Autobots, with our planet nearly sacrificed as a prize.

Dozens more could be named but the point is this: When our world is in great stress (as it seems always to be, with the rise of aggressive international terrorism and enormous financial crises), apocalyptic productions of stage, screen, or sentence proliferate. Doomsday books roll off the presses, television shows like *Fringe* or *Eleventh Hour* or *The 4400* replicate and disaster movies multiply. Even *2012* loomed on our horizon as the year that the ancient Mayan calendar ended, an event that called for scary exploitation.

Apocalyptic visioning is nothing new. Every civilization, and especially those that were dying, has had end-time doomsayers. Even the Bible shows evidence of that. When the Assyrians stormed through Israel and devastated it in 722 BC, little Judah to the south was engulfed in a cloud of moody and frightening prophecies, including dozens collected in Isaiah's volume. The book of Revelation would serve much the same purpose in the early Christian church as the early days of power and glory gave way to the darkening killing fields of persecution.

The biblical apocalyptic visions never end in total annihilation. These nasty times are always the gateway to salvation, restoration, and renewal. Into this tragedy-engulfed world, however, shines a light. It is a light of grace, a light of hope, a light of salvation, a light of transformation. It is, of course, a divine light, whose source is none other than Yahweh, the God of Israel and the Lord of the nations. But this marvelous light of hope and restoration, on the apocalyptic battlefields of our world, is prismed through the faith community of God's peculiar people.

The message is clear. Earth will not end with either a bang or a whimper, as T.S. Eliot presumed, but with the blazing light of divine love, which will restore, renew, and resuscitate all things until God's good intentions are finally experienced by all. Whatever apocalyptic doom holds sway in any society is only the prelude to God's next great act of re-creation, which will produce a great dance of recreation among all of humanity.

The symbolic language of the Old Testament gains specificity in its New Testament realizations, of course. First of all, the prophetic "Day of the Lord" was split in two, so that the blessings of realized eschatology could begin with the Messiah's first coming as a baby in Bethlehem, while the catastrophic divine cleansing would wait until a later date. Secondly, through Jesus and the church that lived in the power of his Spirit, some of the shades and shadows of humanity's self-destructive trammeling are pushed back and pockets of glory shine around every congregation that throbs with the radiance of heaven.

The religion of the Bible is predicated on the assumption that all of experiential reality had a beginning and was brought into being by a creator and that this deity desires an ongoing relationship with the worlds that exist. More particularly, this

God nurtures a special longing to engage the human race as the unique and crowning species within the grand complexity of molecules and moons, fish and fowl, galaxies and granite, emotions and electrons.

But in its understanding of this ongoing arm wrestling of creator and creature, biblical religion is deeply rooted in human history. This expression of values and ideas is not merely a moral construct that makes life easier. Nor is it a set of centering exercises that will keep the imminent more fully tuned to the transcendent. Instead, the story put forward in biblical literature is that the creatures of earth have lost their ability to apprehend or understand their Creator, and that the deity must necessarily take not only the first but also many recurring steps in an effort to reconnect with them. So revelation is a concept involving action and content. The deity must somehow interrupt the normal course of affairs in human existence in a way that will catch our attention. When we have stopped to notice or ponder or even step back in fright, there must be some information that becomes accessible to us in a way that allows and encourages us to rethink the meaning of all things.

It is in this sense that we need to understand the power of today's scripture reading. There is a new star shining in the sky. Why? Because the world is dark and expectations are limited. Only a new revelation can help the Magi or us find meaning. Not only that, but the darkness is so thick and bleak that Herod is himself completely taken over by it and willing to perpetuate murder in hopes of keeping the darkness all to himself!

The literature of the Bible is rooted in two major divine interruptions into human history — first, the events of the Exodus and Sinai Covenant that created Israel as a missional nation, and then later the unusual and unrepeatable incarnation of deity in the person of Jesus Christ. All of the literature of the Bible is gathered around these two redemptive events and their implications. For this reason, the Pentateuch and the gospels are the critical elements shaping the biblical religion. They are not codes of law or wise ethical teachings from a distinguished school of thought; they are the documents articulating an unusual intrusion of divine will into the human arena for the threefold purpose of actively transforming lives by redemptive transactions, teaching the Creator's original worldview, and establishing a missional community that will live out and disseminate those perspectives.

If the Bible is to have any ongoing religious value, its two historical nodes of divine redemptive activity must be taken seriously. Stripped of the Exodus/Sinai Covenant or of the redemptive divinity of Jesus, the Bible makes little sense. Suddenly its moral codes are no better than others that have been formed and articulated at various points throughout history, its pilgrimage images are little different from other quests for significance and the sacred, and its personalities become only another bunch of interesting heroes and drifters who give moral lessons through their flawed frolicking.

If there is a God, and if that God wished to reclaim by creatorial right a relationship with those brought into being as an extension of the divine fellowship and heavenly energy, the Bible makes a good deal of sense. It is a collection of covenant documents that trace the divine redemptive mission through two stages: its early history in locating a transformed community at the crossroads of human society in order to be seen and desired, and its later expression through an expanding and transforming presence in every culture that tells the story of God along with the other tales of life. Paul finds himself helping the faith community of the Old Testament transition into this New Age of mission. This is his special calling, and it is directly related to the great "mystery" of God's intentions that have been hovering over us from the beginning.

Like the rest of literature, the Bible can be ignored, misread, or improperly used. But like the best of literature, when allowed to speak from its own frame of reference and respected as a collection of documents that are inherently seeking to enhance human life rather than deviously attempting to exploit it, the Bible is truly, in a very powerful and exciting way, the Word of God.

The theme of Jesus' royal identity is consistently emphasized throughout Matthew's gospel, rooted directly in the covenant Yahweh made with David in 2 Samuel 7. There the themes of God's house and David's house came together in powerful symmetry. David wished to build a house for God now that Israel was settled in the Promised Land. While God appreciated the appropriate desire on David's part, through the prophet Nathan, God communicated that it would be David's son, a man of peace, who would take up that honor and responsibility. But because David's heart and desires were in the right place, God made a return commitment to him. God would build a royal "house" out of David's descendants, and there would always be one of his sons ruling as king over God's people.

Although the intervening years since the Babylonian Exile had not allowed Jewish self-determination until very recently and even though this new small freedom of the Jews failed to follow the Davidic dynasty in restoring the throne in Jerusalem, Matthew makes it clear that Jesus is indeed the one who will fulfill, now and forever, God's commitment to David. This he communicates powerfully in the opening chapters of the gospel.

First, Matthew makes sure his readers connect Jesus' birth to David's lineage in 1:1-17, including a special division of the years to indicate that God was about to act once again in salvation, and Jesus showed up at precisely the right time.

Second, Jesus' birth is as marvelous, mysterious, and miraculous as were the births of Isaac and Samson and Samuel, great patriarchs and deliverers for ancient Israel. Jesus is another in the line of God's special ambassadors to bring about the salvation of the people.

Third, when Jesus is born, nations far beyond these tiny borders recognize that an international ruler of transcendent significance has come to earth. Matthew alone records this story of the Magi, not to make us speculate about who they were or how many came or even what their names might have been. The essential point is clear: While in Jesus' own homeland there remain bloody contests for local rule, within the international community the quest to finally find a king of consequence has been divinely channeled toward baby Jesus. The signs have been posted in the heavens.

The message of Epiphany Sunday is not about the mystery of the Magi but about the divine revelation. God makes it abundantly clear that God is interrupting human affairs to bring a salvation that we cannot devise on our own. Jesus is not merely one among the many good religious leaders who have happened along through time; he is the Creator's last and greatest attempt to bring us home. Christianity is not just one dimension of the multifaceted religious landscape that surrounds us in a pluralistic world; it holds the core doctrines that bring about the salvation of all.

Epiphany is not about the marvel of seeing potential in a tiny baby. It is a reminder that the religion of the Bible is exclusive in its origins and in its message of salvation. This does not make Christianity petty or prideful; it simply means that once you know the larger story of God's redemptive purposes toward our world, it is a privilege to share the good news about Jesus!

Light is the key theme today and the revelation it cast into dark places. Matthew's specially selected story of the coming of the Magi is a reminder that the Creator has not done all of this in some secret corner but, in the very religions of our world, has left vestiges of human groping through blindness for a divine redemption. Let the light shine! Shine, Jesus, shine! Amen.

**Baptism of Our Lord**
**Epiphany 1**
**Ordinary Time 1**
**Luke 3:15-17, 21-22**

# *Here Comes Jesus!*

The 1995 film *Waterworld* projected humanity into a post-global-warming world where the polar ice caps had melted and civilization drowned beneath the waves. Survivors sailed and scavenged, always threatened by other pirates on the high seas. But lingering in the whispered nighttime tale-telling were legends of dry land and a return to humanity's original paradise.

The threats, images, and hopes of *Waterworld* come alive in a biblical fashion on this Baptism Sunday. The baptism of Jesus is our central focus, but it happens under the strangely compelling ministry of wild and woolly John. First of all, John's identity and ministry are directly connected to the prophetic message of ancient Israel (vv. 2-3). In this way, Jesus' own life and actions are declared to be the fulfillment of divine planning and purpose. Jesus is not a new figure suddenly sprung upon the scene with no context; he is a fully endorsed Messiah who appears emerging out of long-finished script.

Second, John is a riveting figure. He is countercultural. No one should suppose that anything connected with John is part of the status quo. He looks wild. He acts wildly. Yet he is not insane or delirious. In fact, he is most rationally in tune with things as they should be, and therefore those who have been lulled into the complacency of that time experience through him a wake-up call to reclaim what is good, right, and essential about life.

Third, John's ministry of baptism gives his message public urgency. It is one thing for folks to hear a rousing sermon or political speech and then to go out into the next work day with it only lingering as water-cooler conversation. It is quite another for people to respond to a public "altar call" and to be visibly identified with a change-of-life cause. Because John demanded that his hearers take physical action after hearing the message of repentance and devotion, his followers suddenly became a zealous missionary enterprise. They were not only convicted; they were convinced and convincing.

In this light, it made sense for Jesus to begin his public ministry by getting baptized by John. This provided a serious, public jump-start for Jesus' own ministry, which was every bit as challenging as John's. Furthermore, God thundered a divine confirmation, speaking a royal endorsement from the heavens. Luke gets it right and spells it out simply: Here comes Jesus, grounded in the kingdom vision of Israel's past, inducted by a larger-than-life prophet, and commissioned directly by the voice of the Creator. Just wait until you read the rest of the story!

I remember a new gospel hit when I was a teen with words taken from a classic spiritual out of mind and reworked for the Jesus-people generation. We sang it with gusto:

> *Here comes Jesus, see Him walking on the water,*
> *He'll lift you up and He'll help you to stand;*
> *Oh, here comes Jesus,*
> *He's the Master of the waves that roll.*
> *Here comes Jesus, let him take your hand.*
>       — "Here Comes Jesus" (public domain)

By themselves, the words say little and reveal less. But like the coding of what we used to call "negro spirituals," there is a whole world standing behind the slim pickings of the text itself. For one thing, Jesus has to enter our world from outside, since the status quo is awfully messed up and somebody better come and do something about it. Second, when Jesus arrives, in whatever time or place, he comes with unusual power, walking on water and taming storms. Third, we are fallen and weak, needing someone and something outside of ourselves to heal our wounds and restore our dignity.

In our fevered passionate chantings of the new music over against the old stuff of the church that no longer spoke to us or for us, we were shouting the gospel. This is precisely what is taking place when Jesus comes to be baptized. Luke pictures for us what it was like to see Jesus coming down to the Jordan where he was first publicly identified as the Savior, not only by his cousin John, but also by the divine pronouncement and visible anointing. Here comes Jesus... and the world has never been the same!

"You've got to see *Avatar*," wrote a friend of mine, some years ago. A doctoral student in philosophical studies who breathes skepticism, my friend is not known for gushing, particularly at Hollywood productions. Yet *Avatar* had fired up his jets because, he said, it told the truth. Not the accurate truth about historical events, or the warm truth about relationships, or the scientific truth about exploration and discovery, but the truth about meaning, existence, life, and about God.

The movie industry sells a lot of the fluff and mediocrity that audiences crave because we want quick-fix emotional escapes. But in Hollywood's squalid mix there are "utopias." Thomas More coined that term for his 1516 social critique, combining the Greek words for "no" and "place" to speak of a Neverland that we desperately want but cannot find.

*Avatar* brings a lump to our throats because what springs to life in 3-D splendor is a utopia that meets five of our hearts' longings:

- It criticizes our current world's crass materialism.
- It inspires in us the contours of a world where truer, purer values guide us.

- It cleanses us by setting in stark contrast the baser drives we too often express and the higher moral values that can shape us.
- It calls to us with the voice of kind wisdom that resonates with our deepest feelings, beckoning us home.
- It portrays characters who make the journey ahead of us, giving us hope that we can follow them.

Although More's *Utopia* doesn't grab me quite the way it did others in his age, I understand why they were thrilled. I have my own list of utopias that come to mind when people ask about "best books" and "favorite movies." While I can't always explain my choices, this I know: Something of the coming kingdom of God whistles through them, yanking me into eternity, even for a brief moment. It is indeed like poet and cancer victim Donna Hoffman wrote in her waning months: "My feet stumble, but ah, how my heart can soar!"

This is the message this morning. Luke helps us understand the transformational moment when eternity stepped into time at the coming of Jesus, and a new world order was born. Here comes Jesus! Amen.

**Epiphany 2
Ordinary Time 2
John 2:1-11**

# *Becoming What We Were Meant to Be*

Mine is a family of book lovers. Early on, my wife and I encouraged our daughters to read and bought them books we thought they'd enjoy. It was no surprise to us that in their younger years the girls often chose books by the look of their covers. But as they grew to love the quality of the stories they read, the appearance of a book became less important. Now they understand that "you can't judge a book by its cover."

English is full of proverbs like that — still waters run deep, beauty is only skin deep, looks can be deceiving, good things come in small packages. We learn quickly to distrust appearances, because too often they don't tell the whole story.

Still, it's nice when the cover of a book is of the same wonderful quality as that of the story inside. I have some leather-bound, gold-embossed books I appreciate as much for their intelligent construction as for their inspiring character. So it is with today's gospel reading. John's memories of Jesus' first days of public ministry show a man called and destined to be nothing less than the incarnate Son of God who helps others find their identity and destiny as well.

The gospel of John is unlike any other biblical or extra-biblical writing. Since it has the most literary kinship with the synoptic gospels, in that it rehearses elements from the life and teachings of Jesus and forms part of the "gospel quartet" of the New Testament. But even a quick read will show significant differences from these other uniquely Christian writings. First, it has a global philosophic introduction that places the story of Jesus in a comprehensive cosmological frame of reference. Second, it is often more cryptic in its conversational narratives than are the other gospels, making it harder to understand how or why some of these dialogues could have taken place. Third, while it acknowledges that Jesus did many miracles, it reports only seven of these during his public ministry and elevates the significance of these few by attaching to them deeper and more complex secondary meanings. Fourth, there are extended monologues by Jesus scattered throughout the pages of John's gospel, which are mystical and doctrinal and have no clear parallel to the manner of Jesus' teachings or conversations as recorded by the synoptics. In short, the fourth gospel is a wild ride in a theme park of its own.

Yet it is also so homey and comfortable that elements of it are like old slacks and shirts worn easily. The Greek language, through which the text is communicated, is basic and simple so that even beginner students can quickly read it. Many of its teachings, from the lips of Jesus, have become the inextricable metaphors and motifs by which we know him and ourselves — the good shepherd, the light of the world, the resurrection and the life, the vine, and so forth. Some of the conversations Jesus had with others are recorded in a manner that makes us feel as if we were the only ones they were penned for, and we are always sitting next to Jesus again when we read them. Even our Christian theology and worldview has been so shaped, over the centuries, by themes from this document that we cannot separate it from us or imagine Christianity apart from these 21 chapters. The gospel according to John is a key element of biblical faith.

Although its literary development is markedly different from that of the synoptic gospels, there is a very clear pattern to John's rehearsal of thought and portrayal of Jesus' activities and teachings in this gospel. A significant transition in referential time takes place between chapters 12 and 13. This change is further accentuated by the grouping of all of Jesus' "miraculous signs," as John calls them, into the first twelve chapters. For these reasons the first part of John's gospel is often called "The Book of Signs," while the last part wears well the name, "The Book of Glory." A highly significant prologue opens the gospel (1:1-18), and an epilogue, perhaps written by another party and added after the initial gospel was completed (ch. 21), brings it to a close.

The curious strength of that powerfully creative literary skeleton can be found in our gospel reading today. Notice that the prologue summary is completed in the first fourteen verses, followed by John's brief authorial nod in 1:15-18. Then comes a quick series of vignettes that proceed by marked "days." The work of John the Baptist is highlighted in the first "day" (1:19-28), the public identification of Jesus is the point of the second "day" (1:29-34), the welcoming home of the first disciples marks the third "day" (1:35-43), and the beginning of the mission shared by Jesus and his followers is the focus of the fourth "day" (1:44-51). John's chronology then places Jesus' first "miraculous sign" (turning water into wine at the marriage feast in Cana) three days later (2:1), thus declaring that it takes place on the "sabbath" of these initial seven days, and the celebration of God's good pleasure in the creation.

In other words, the close calendar watching that marks John's initial scenes is very important. Like the days of creation in Genesis (to which John makes a very clear connection as the gospel opens), divine light shines in the darkness on day 1 (John the Baptist's testimony as he hovers above the waters of the Jordan), the firmaments are distinguished in day 2 (Jesus is from above, we are from below), a home is made for use on day 3 (like the earth of human above in the creation listing), and the bearer of light begins to warm the world to life on day 4.

So today's scripture reading needs to be read in tandem with Genesis 1, a fitting exercise at the beginning of this year. The point John is making as he opens the story of Jesus is that in a world compromised and darkened by sin, the light of eternity begins to shine again, and we who were created for life begin to stir again with divine glory. Jesus, of course, is the first fruits at the head of the new humanity, but we are invited along in the transformation, becoming once again what we were meant to be.

Such a focused scope and grand vision reminds me of Victor Hugo's greatest novel. He called his masterpiece, *Les Miserables*, a religious work. So it is. The story echoes the gospel message at nearly every turn.

The main character, Jean Valjean, has been beaten hard by the cruel twists of fate. He has seen the sham of hypocrisy on all sides. So he casts the name of the Lord to the ground like a curse. What does God know of him, and what does it matter?

Imprisoned for stealing bread to feed his family and re-sentenced by the vindictive will of his jailer, Jean Valjean finally manages to escape. On his first night of freedom, he stays with a bishop, who treats him well. But behind Jean Valjean's thankful mask is the cunning face of a thief, for the bishop has many valuables.

In the early morning hours, Jean Valjean steals away with some silver plates. When his suspicious appearance brings him under arrest, he is forced to face the bishop again, charged with new crimes.

Then the miracle of grace occurs. For in Jean Valjean's eyes the bishop sees something that begs forgiveness and hopes for mercy. Instead of taking revenge, the bishop declares that the silver dishes were a gift to Jean Valjean. In fact, he says Jean Valjean forgot to take the two silver candlesticks he had also given him.

In an instant, the bishop declares Jean Valjean innocent and gives him back his life. But with this gift of forgiveness, he commissions Jean Valjean to bring Christ to others. The rest of Jean Valjean's life becomes a testimony of one who is made new in the grace of divine love. He becomes what he was meant to be.

Not only that, but Jean Valjean spends the rest of his life helping his young charge, Cosette, find love and a good marriage. The redeemed becomes the redeemer. The one who has seen the light becomes the light of life for others.

While the parallels can only be drawn so far, there are powerful images that are repeated when trying to figure out the deep meanings of life. John, in telling us this story about Jesus, does more than send up a tabloid headline: "Local Boy Turns Water into Wine!" He helps us see the broad sweep of human history in which all our best efforts at marriages and families, societies, and civilization come undone at the seams because of our weak and wicked ways. Only when someone from outside the system names our disease and offers a vaccine against the ravages of original sin will we realize just how deeply we have been stuck in the well of our despair.

Charles Darwin grew up in a Christian home, yet later in life he rejected Christianity's hold on him. How did this loss of faith happen? Here's the explanation from his autobiography: "I gradually came to disbelieve in Christianity... disbelief crept over me at a very slow rate but at last it was complete. The rate was so slow that I felt no distress."

Darwin's words could have fallen from the pages of many diaries. His experience is the same as many in the church who lose their faith. They lose it because they don't use it. Because they never do anything with it. Because they have become less than they truly are.

Jesus' first miraculous sign at the wedding of a distant relative in Cana that he helped his mother cater was a billboard on humanity's journey to even darker places. "Turn here!" it cried. "Light is in that direction! Follow the young man, Mary's son, because if you do, the celebration will return to the party!"

Do you believe it or has your complacency with the dull drabness of life in the shadows made you think, with Charles Darwin, that "ho" and "hum" are the only real words that matter?

Wake up! Get excited! Drink the wine and become again what you were meant to be! Amen.

**Epiphany 3**
**Ordinary Time 3**
**Luke 4:14-21**

# *Creating Community the Hard Way*

In his book on civility, *A World Waiting to Be Born*, M. Scott Peck mused that community was lacking in our world and hard to recover. Perhaps, because of the time that we are forced to spend with one another at work, we might bring about a little of it there, he said. Maybe even in marriages and families, if we count the true cost of divorce. But Peck was quite certain that community could never happen in churches. After all, he said, community requires that we spend time together and that we choose to work through our differences with one another. However, church life in North America, according to Peck, had become another consumerist enterprise with little corners of the Sunday cafeteria serving up differing musical and message morsels to taste, and Christians grazing briefly in politeness before they re-isolate themselves from the threat of community.

Unfortunately, Peck's prophetic perceptions are too much on target. That's why when Jesus goes home to preach, Jesus makes it a message about the "Year of Jubilee."

After my first year in seminary, my home congregation in rural Minnesota asked me to preach on a Sunday morning. Luke's story of Jesus heading home to Nazareth haunted me in the weeks leading up to the momentous occasion. Who was I to think that I could walk into the worship sanctuary of my boyhood community and suddenly proclaim the word of God to my parents and their peers, not to mention my friends and classmates who knew me too well to take me seriously? Would I be pelted with overripe tomatoes and rotten eggs for my efforts at "exhorting" or "proclaiming" or whatever it was that I would try to do from that familiar pulpit? Would I be laughed out of the building before I had even begun, despicable in my over-indulgent earnestness? Or, as happened to the Jesus I pledged to serve, would piles of stones be stacked at the doors, ready for my departing "blessing," just before lynching?

Well, family and friends back home were kind, not taking a lesson from the murmuring mutterers in Nazareth some twenty centuries earlier. What made things turn so differently for Jesus in his hometown? The passage for the day, from Isaiah 61, was marvelous, one of the great testimonies of divine initiative written by the most poetically gifted among the great prophets. Jesus' message was short and sweet, certainly not preventing folks from getting home before the Sabbath roast was overdone. Even the first responses were strong affirmations of the boy wonder who grew up among us (v. 22). Yet when Jesus added a few explanatory notes, the place exploded with vitriolic bitterness, and mob frenzy strove to end the service with murder (vv. 23-30).

These notes about the response of Jesus' neighbors and friends to his first attempt at preaching help us understand the meaning of this moment. It was not merely a familiar rabbinical student exercising his limited eloquence for the first time with the hometown crowd. According to Luke, it was an occasion of incredible divine revelation. Two things, in particular, contributed to its significance. First, there was the text itself. Although written long after Israel's wilderness beginnings at the foot of Mount Sinai, the word of God that came to the prophet Isaiah was deeply rooted in the covenant-making ceremony that happened back then. Leviticus 25 outlined the greatest of all the festivals that shaped Israel's calendar. It was the "Year of Jubilee," a once-in-a-lifetime event when lands would go back to original families, debts would be forgiven, families would be restored, slaves would be freed, and Yahweh would provide enough natural growth from the land that no farming need be done for two years. The whole country could live out a twelve-month party.

Unfortunately, according to the rest of the Old Testament records, the grand "Year of Jubilee" never took place. Purportedly scheduled every fifty years, it was always delayed by circumstances or forgotten by busyness or ignored by consumerism or set aside as inconvenient. By the time of Judah's exile in 586 BC, the prophets have begun to talk about the removal of the people from the land as God's way of making certain that the long-neglected "Year of Jubilee" grand Sabbath would finally get its due. If the celebration and rest would not happen with the elect community around, it would happen without them.

The word of the Lord that came through Isaiah in what we call chapter 61 was a poetic visioning of what things would look like when the "Year of Jubilee" was finally celebrated. The Spirit of God would energize all, and hope and healing and happiness would flood through the settled territories until no need would go unmet, no tear would fall without turning into a smile, no call of hunger would go unanswered by feasting, and no alienation or marginalization would be unaddressed by the best of community-building. One day, some day, maybe Yahweh would come and finally bring in the "Year of Jubilee."

So when Jesus came home to the synagogue in Nazareth, it was a wonderful thing to hear his voice intone these great promises and prophetic hopes. But the kicker was his short application: "Today this scripture is fulfilled in your hearing." It was a declaration that he was bringing in the "Year of Jubilee." That was either a gross overstatement, since no human had the ability to make such a transcendent event happen, or a mighty egoistical sacrilegious boast, delusional in making Jesus out to be God! Either way, the nice text was given a bad twist in a crudely exaggerated sermonic application. So they would think, not knowing what we believe about Jesus and his work, from our vantage point.

Second, another rub came in the way that the text from Isaiah was cut short by Jesus when he read it. He failed to read the last clause, "and the day of vengeance of our God." This phrase was typically used as part of the explanation of why the "Year of Jubilee" had not been and could not be celebrated. Other nations prevented it. There was always a political threat that kept the people of God from following through on the magic of these promised months, making it impossible for Israel/Judah to live out the pleasure of this festival. Only if God would come with vengeance and strike our enemies down in disgrace and disaster would we be able to truly enjoy the "Year of Jubilee."

When Jesus simply declared that the year had come in himself and that no punishments were to be meted out on the Romans, the whole matter took a new spin that left the cherished prejudices panting for something Jesus wouldn't give. God was bringing the blessings of the messianic age through Jesus without necessarily pounding Jewish enemies to a pulp. The savory taste of vengeance was removed from the equation, and now somebody had to pay. Let's take it out on Jesus! Though this moment of mob hysteria may have seemed like an anomaly, in the months ahead it would become the very movement that would finally bring about Jesus' excruciating execution. Which, in turn, would actually usher in the very things that Jesus was preaching about. How ironic!

One of M. Scott Peck's earlier books, *The Different Drum*, analyzes community and how it evolves. There are four stages to developing deep community, according to Peck: pseudo-community, conflict, chaos, and true community. The first is our surface friendliness in group settings because we are nice people. Most churches are probably at least an expression of this. But bring any conflict, and tensions flare. At this point, according to Peck, we have the options of staying together and working things through or going our separate ways. God and the Bible point in the former direction, but our experientialist society mostly pushes us the other way, because we want pleasure, not pain.

The committed few who grapple with conflict and come out on the other side often suddenly experience chaos. We've stayed together, but what's the point? Who's in charge around here anyway? Who will validate our raggedy band? And without clear lines of authority or comforting leadership, too often "things fall apart," as Yeats said in his famous poem and Achebe diagrammed in his novel by that name.

If community is a divine gift, something profoundly wonderful can happen to and for those who cling, hope, and pray. This beautiful outcome is the church, the body of Christ, the family of faith, the people of God, the Year of Jubilee in all of its fullness. Can you see it? Are you part of it?

How will you respond to the first sermon of Jesus? A dear friend once explained it like this: In a dream he saw a marvelous apparatus of yellow silk billowing in the breezes next to a cliff. It was a transportation device of some kind, though he couldn't see either and engine or supports. Like a magical tent, it floated in space.

Inside was a man whose face seemed so familiar and friendly that my friend knew immediately this was an intimate acquaintance. However, he could not seem to remember how they were associated, or the man's name. The man, with a smile of warmth, invited him to step off the cliff into the contrivance to be carried on a delightful journey in the yellow tent.

My friend was so intrigued by the device itself that he wanted to try it on his own. He wanted to pilot the magical airship, so when he entered the craft he fought the man for control and pushed him out onto the cliff. Unfortunately, just as my friend felt the power of flight swell in his commanding grasp, the entire yellow tent began to collapse on itself and plummet to disaster below. No matter what he did, my friend could not make the "machine" fly. He cried for help and suddenly the man he had pushed out reappeared at his side. In that exact moment the airship began to billow and slow its freefall. Soon they were soaring together.

Without a further thought my friend knew that the strangely familiar man was Jesus. He also knew why Jesus said to him, "Don't you know that the power to fly is not found in the 'machine' nor in your skills as a pilot but in me?"

None of us begins to soar in life until we meet Jesus. As the whole Bible declares, it is all about Jesus. Amen.

**Epiphany 4**
**Ordinary Time 4**
**Luke 4:21-30**

# *Prophet*

Ernest Hemmingway wrestled for years just to get one sentence right. He may have become a great novelist over time, but it was not something immediately obvious about him in his younger years. The voice came slowly and was heard only tentatively at the start of his journalistic career. Yet when the muse finally spoke with power, people listened closely and carefully and with interest.

A prophet's voice has that power on us. In our noisy world, where Bethlehem has become bedlam and electronic devices prevent us from wandering far from music, news, or serialized entertainment, it is hard to hear a clear prophetic voice. When it happens, now and again, heads turn and conversation is stilled. The same words used by everyone else are piled up by the prophet, yet they sound different. They sing. They dance. They punch. They swirl. They lift. They probe.

As we read in today's scripture, people may push the prophet away. "It's only rhetoric!" "Fancy words, that's all!" "Nice talk, but we have to live in the real world!" In fact, responding well to a prophet's message is not usually a natural human trait. Not even when the prophet is Jesus or the message as hopeful as the brief one he delivered that day in his hometown synagogue.

Yet those who receive the words of the prophet with uncensored ears and wistful hearts are rewarded. For a few brief moments in time the voice of God resonates. Cataracts melt from eyes and fear dissolves in the mind. Sight is restored, vision refocused, lives are mended, and hope leads the way. This is why Moses promised ancient Israel that God would always provide prophecy for them, leading eventually to the voice of the great one who would proclaim loudly the goodness of heaven. This is why the apostle Paul's voice was still requested by the Corinthian congregation after he left town, even when restless arguing sometimes muted his authority among them. This is why even the demons shouted when Jesus passed by, hoping to embarrass him into silence. But the prophet's voice cannot be stilled. That is why we preach today.

There is a great story about the dissonance and power of a prophetic voice in John F. Kennedy's Pulitzer Prize winning book *Profiles in Courage*. It is found in the chapter on George W. Norris titled "I Have Come Home to Tell You the Truth." Kennedy narrates the story of a Nebraska congressman who had the fortitude to take unpopular stands during the hoopla leading up to America's involvement in World War II, and who was willing to go back to his home state to explain his very unpopular actions in town hall meetings where his own political party refused support or endorsement. Norris did not apologize for his political choices, which were opposed by his constituents; he merely told the people whom he represented that if he had been trusted by them to act on their behalf, he had pledged always to do the right thing. News reports and editorials had blasted his unpopular stance against government and business warmongering and panic arousal by labeling him unpatriotic. Even the Nebraska governor got into the act and hinted that he might ask the state legislature to begin recall proceedings.

Norris declared that if it was the will of the people, he would gladly step down from office. But first, he said, he wanted to explain why his views had developed the way they did, and how these had influenced his voting record. He would return to Nebraska and meet face-to-face with his constituents. No one supported him in this politically suicidal endeavor. His own party refused to schedule or publicize the meetings he had in mind. The first, in Lincoln, gave the appearance of throwing a maimed chicken into a pen of ravenous and angry pit bulls. Patriotic fervor had ignited a boiling caldron of venom aimed at destroying him on the spot. But Norris quietly began by saying, "I have come home to tell you the truth." Then, as intrigued voters started to listen, the congressman poured out his heart in prophetic tones of vision, justice, morality, and honesty. When he finished, the crowd and even the press loudly endorsed his actions and sent him back to Washington for many more years.

Every society wants its scapegoats, just as every people is looking for a prophet. The two are very closely related, as Plato reflected in *The Republic*. Moses himself was a prophet who more than once became the target of frustrated Israel and a good number of coup attempts, even from his own family. When Moses gave his farewell address, he assured the Israelites, in Deuteronomy 18, that God would provide future prophetic leadership to fill the void left by Moses' own imminent departure. Israel needed a prophet, if it was to fulfill its divine mission and purpose. So it is no wonder that when young Jesus comes home to preach and delivers a prophet's message, scapegoating and admiration dance a tango in the neighborhood crowd.

Of course, opening this door of prophetic expectation served as a blanket invitation to charlatans and self-aggrandizing tyrants who would vie, throughout Israel's history, as contenders for the office left too long vacant. Some would be kings who cared not for the covenant mediated by Moses; others would flash their mail-order degrees from slimy schools of spirituality and claim these as prophetic license. "Watch out!" Moses commanded. The true prophet who comes in my place and speaks for Yahweh will be known because he will tell the truth.

It is no wonder that centuries later the remnant of Israel, now reduced to the bickering residue of Judah, were still looking for the great prophet. When Jesus came, speaking with honesty, speaking with clarity, speaking with no pretense, the crowds began asking anew, "Is this the prophet?"

Philip Yancey remembers a powerful Sunday evening during the socially disruptive 1960s when a visiting speaker came to preach at his church. Angered by the obvious racism of the congregation and its poor track record of assistance to the area's needy, the preacher began by saying, "God d**n!" In the shocked silence he went on: "You will probably never allow me to preach here again. Right now you are terribly offended by my words. But you take offense at something I've said, while you continue to be blind to the offense you give in the name of Christ by the racism of your actions and your scandalous disregard for the needy nearby you."

We can imagine what people were talking about in Nazareth. Jesus bursts upon the scene in Galilee like a whirlwind. Jesus bounced restlessly around the Jezreel Valley with fierce intensity, preaching, teaching, healing, and casting out demons. Almost immediately Jesus is the new religious sensation, the talking point for all social commentators.

Jesus is also the familiar stranger for folks in the north country. He is the man who lives down the hall, yet remains an enigma to his own family. Those around him recognize Jesus as the boy who grew up in the next town, even while people of the area are disturbed by the striking power and authority that lingers in the air around Jesus wherever he goes. It quickly becomes obvious that Jesus' own disciples don't really know him, and we are not that different from them. It takes a demonic spirit to call out what the crowds are not willing to admit: "I know who you are — the holy one of God!"

I think of this every time I teach a college course called "Which Jesus?" I take my students through Jaroslav

Pelikan's book, *Jesus through the Centuries* (Yale, 1999), and the writings of the New Testament. Using these as starting points, we reflect on the variety of ways in which people have thought about Jesus and continue to reflect on him. The major assignment I give is for each student to write a paper that requires them to talk with their parents about how Mom and Dad view Jesus. Invariably I get some papers still wet with tears from students who never before knew the Jesus of their parents' religious devotions. Too long they had passed by one another snickering at the religious folly of others while never having to face the question of Jesus' identity themselves.

Luke wants us to face the challenge early in our encounter with Jesus through his gospel. We may dislike the man. We may revile him. We may try to suck up to him or wheedle him like some magical genie but ignore him we may not do. Otherwise even the demons will cry out in awe-filled recognition.

Why did Jesus seem to have authority that was lacking among the usual teachers of the law in his day? Part of what people sensed was likely the divine Spirit oozing through Jesus' personality, commanding attention simply because it is impossible to ignore God when pitched that close at hand. But probably Jesus' authority had to do also with the nature of his teaching. The scribes and teachers of the law were careful not to equate their words or interpretations as either equal to or taking precedence over the written word of God. So, at most, they could rise to the social level of "rabbi," "my teacher." They remained interpreters of the divine text, not prophets revealing a new message from God.

Jesus, however, was not limited in this manner. He could interpret the given text with appropriate confidence and also declare a new word of heavenly testimony. Because cult leaders do this all the time, there was a sense about whether the early following that surrounded Jesus was exactly that:

cultish. But Jesus has something going for him that no Jim Jones, Charles Manson, or David Koresh would ever possess; he is, in fact, the Son of God.

While those in Nazareth may not have known what to do with Jesus, Jesus certainly knows what to do with us. As we mob him, seeking a way to quiet his prophetic voice, Jesus slips through our mayhem, ready to fulfill what will become his most powerful prophetic message. As Edwin Markham so elegantly gave voice to Jesus' message:

> *He drew a circle that shut me out —*
> *Heretic, rebel, a thing to flout.*
> *But love and I had the wit to win:*
> *We drew a circle that took him in.*
> Can we receive that word from our great prophet today?
> — *Outwitted* (public domain)

Amen.

**Transfiguration of Our Lord**
**(Last Sunday after Epiphany)**
**Luke 9:28-36 (37-43)**

# *Glow in the Dark*

The story of Marie Curie is more fascinating than most fictional novels. Born Polish, and to a family that lost everything in the political uprisings of the nineteenth century, Marie found her identity at the University of Paris. She was married to Pierre, a man who treated her as an equal in scientific investigations, and together they shared a Nobel prize for the discovery of the causes of radioactivity. When Pierre was killed in a traffic accident, Marie was invited by the university to occupy his chair as the first female professor of the school. Marie went on to distinguish herself in many other ways that include naming two new-found elements (polonium and radium), achieving another Nobel prize, raising a daughter who would distinguish herself in scientific investigations and earn a Nobel prize of her own, and founding or equipping several research schools, even while running on the edge of personal scandal and international political intrigues.

Madame Curie died in 1934 as a direct result of prolonged and unprotected exposure to the very substances she "gave" to the world. She loved to carry around her test tubes of radioactive materials, remarking often about the lovely bluish-green glow they emitted.

There is a kind of allegorical parallel between Curie's story and today's scripture passage. It revolves around a report of eerie glowing that happens when people experience direct encounters with the divine. The outcomes, of course, bring life instead of death, but there is that mesmerizing "glow-in-the-dark" quality about it all. On this Transfiguration

Sunday, heaven's radiance still shines in tangible ways, by way of Jesus, and through his body, the church.

While the synoptic gospels (Matthew, Mark, and Luke) seem at first glance to have little obvious literary structure, all three actually espouse a similar macro form that, if pictured, would look something like a huge suspension bridge, perhaps like the mighty Mackinac that spans the narrows between lakes Superior, Michigan, and Huron. If you have driven it or have seen pictures of it, you know that three long travel segments are separated by two unmistakable uprights. In such a way, in the synoptics, one might think that the three travel segments are: (1) Jesus teaches the crowds about the kingdom of God ("kingdom of heaven" for Matthew), (2) Jesus teaches his disciples about discipleship, and (3) Jesus enters Jerusalem to bring about his passion and resurrection. The "uprights" that form the transition moments between these segments are: (1) the transfiguration and (2) the entry into Jerusalem on the Sunday before his crucifixion. Each "segment" and "upright" plays a critical role in unfolding the meaning and message of Jesus. The opening emphasis on teachings about the kingdom connects Jesus with the whole of Israelite history and prophecy, and explains and explores his personal messianic qualities and role. The transition of the transfiguration indicates that Jesus is now sufficiently known by his disciples, and they must become more privy to the full revelation of his divine character and purpose. Following this exposure, the disciples are more ready to become commissioned witnesses of the Messianic Age that is dawning, but they must understand well their unique role and thus be schooled in the disciplines of discipleship. Finally, when the world is ready for its messiah, Jesus must go to Jerusalem and the temple, for these are the pivotal geographical points on which the whole of God's activity with the world had turned through the Israelite phase of covenant redemption and witness.

The story of the transfiguration, then, tells us a number of critical things. First, it comes immediately on the heels of Peter's great confession of Jesus' identity. Only when Jesus' disciples have begun to understand that their master is not just one among many itinerant rabbis, but truly the promised Messiah, will their ministry of leadership in the age of the church take shape. What happens on the mountain of transfiguration is simply that the testimony of Peter, received by the others and affirmed by Jesus, is modeled before the intimate three. What God placed in Peter's heart to say publicly is now shown in living Technicolor as heaven and earth kiss within the frame of Jesus' body. This is clearly Luke's understanding of the meaning of Jesus' phrase, "I tell you the truth, some who are standing here will not taste death before they see the kingdom of God" (v. 27).

Second, it is important to note that Jesus does not give up his humanity while expressing his divinity, nor become unknown in his divinity so that his humanity is obliterated. The transfiguration is one of the most impressive Christological moments, when the fullness of deity becomes obviously human and the fullness of humanity becomes unquestionably divine. It is a mystery, of course, but it is the reason why the Nicene Creed (birthed out of the Councils of Nicea in 325 and Chalcedon in 451) places the specific limits that it does to our understanding of the natures and person of Jesus.

Third, the appearances of Moses and Elijah are critically instructive. How were Peter, James, and John to know the identity of these two figures who suddenly materialized before them? Probably Jesus told them or the voice from heaven made it obvious. In any case, Moses was the mediator of the Sinai Covenant that was responsible for Israel's national identity and missional purpose on behalf of Yahweh, and Elijah stood at the head of the prophetic line, whose teachings would make the Sinai Covenant a living constitution for the shape of Israel's life. By the time of Jesus, only the "Law" (i.e., the first five books of today's Hebrew Bible, those commonly identified as the books of Moses or the Torah) and the "Prophets" (i.e., the prophetically interpreted histories of Israel found in Samuel and Kings, and the great scrolls of Isaiah, Jeremiah, Ezekiel, and the twelve) were received as authoritative scripture. The "Writings" would be finalized later in the first century. So Moses and Elijah are the fountainheads of the two acknowledged collections of divinely inspired literature. Appearing with Jesus, as they do, Moses and Elijah confirm that the entire word of God points to and is fulfilled in Jesus.

Fourth, Peter's desire to turn the site into a new religious shrine, and Jesus' refusal to allow that to happen is a reminder of the synoptic expression of Jesus' journey. This is only a transitional point, not a conclusion to events. The necessary revelation is not that Jesus has fulfilled the law and the prophets, but he is the fulfillment of the law and the prophets, something that is still underway.

Fifth, the voice from heaven is an external confirmation that this is more than just a dream or hallucinogenic vision. This encounter has substance, and it has a purpose. Now that the three have seen more fully who Jesus is, they carry with them an added responsibility to treat him with appropriate respect and safeguard the mission that he is on. Increased knowledge brings heightened responsibility.

Sixth, immediately after the "mountaintop" exhilaration of the transfiguration, life takes a rather grim turn. We go down the mountain with warm joy in our hearts, only to feel the crush of real life in the valley below. Down here the demons rule. Down here the world is torn by evil. Down here there are pains and torments. Down here the kingdom has not yet become prominent. Moreover, the disciples who were not on the mountain with Jesus do not have any power in themselves to change things. Jesus, of course, has the power, but his range of influence is limited by his conjoined divine and human natures so that he cannot be everywhere at once. He is able to cast out the demon and heal the boy, restoring one small beachhead of the kingdom here, but the other disciples, and those who come to the radiance of the glory of God through them, must still be taught. The transfiguration is a turning point, a transitional statement, but it points to the need for Jesus to finish his work so that its effects might be transferred into the expanding army of grace that would be generalled by these officers-in-training.

A strong New Testament theme is the idea that our world is very dark, Jesus is the light of God penetrating earth's blackness and bleakness, and the Christian church is the lingering glow of divine radiance pushing the transformations of heaven a little further through recessed corners of shame and pain. How are we glowing today?

There is an ancient legend first told by Christians living in the catacombs under the streets of Rome, which pictures the day when Jesus went back to glory after finishing all his work on earth. The angel Gabriel meets Jesus in heaven and welcomes him home. "Lord," he says, "who have you left behind to carry on your work?"

Jesus tells him about the disciples, the little band of fishermen, farmers, and housewives.

"But Lord," says Gabriel, "what if they fail you? What if they lose heart or drop out? What if things get too rough for them, and they let you down?"

"Well," replies Jesus, "then all I've done will come to nothing!"

"But don't you have a backup plan?" Gabriel asks. "Isn't there something else to keep it going, to finish your work?"

"No," says Jesus, "there's no backup plan. The church is it. There's nothing else."

"Nothing else?" says Gabriel. "But what if they fail?"

The early Christians knew Jesus' answer. "They won't fail, Gabriel," he said. "They won't fail!"

Isn't that a marvelous thing? Here are the Christians of Rome, dug into the earth like gophers, tunneling out of sight because of the terrors of Nero up above. They're nothing in that world! They're poor, despised, and insignificant! Yet they know the promise of Jesus: "You won't fail! You're my people, and you won't fail!"

Tony Campolo once told of a friend who was walking through the midway at a county fair when he met a tiny girl. She was carrying a great big fluff of cotton candy on a stick, almost as larger as herself! He said to her, "How can a little girl like you eat all that cotton candy?"

"Well," she said to him, "I'm really much bigger on the inside than I am on the outside!"

So it is with us. On the outside we seem to be nothing, like Jesus' helpless disciples below the mountain of the transfiguration, but on the inside we are as big as the kingdom and the power and the glory of our God.

What would our neighborhood be without us? What would our area be like without the church of Jesus Christ? Where would our nation be without the conscience of the people of God? It's not enough to be anti-abortion; you must be pro-life and remind your community what real life, God's life, is all about! It's not enough to be against immorality; you have to be the conscience of society, turning its thoughts toward love, laughter, and life! It's not enough to protect your own interests; you have to speak out for the welfare of the poor, the disabled, and the oppressed!

There's a marvelous little story tucked away in the pages of Edward Gibbon's seven-volume work, *The Decline and Fall of the Roman Empire*. It tells of a humble little monk named Telemachus living in the farming regions of Asia.

Telemachus had no great ambitions in life. He loved his little garden and tilled it through the changing seasons. But one day in the year 391 he felt a sense of urgency, a call of God's direction in his life. Although he didn't know why, he felt that God wanted him to go to Rome: the heart and soul of the empire. In fact, the feelings of such a call frightened him, but he went anyway, praying along the way for God's direction.

When he finally got to the city, it was in an uproar! The armies of Rome had just come home from the battlefield in victory, and the crowds were turning out for a great celebration. They flowed through the streets like a tidal wave, and Telemachus was caught in their frenzy and carried into the Coliseum.

He had never seen a gladiator contest before, but now his heart sickened. Down in the arena men hacked at each other with swords and clubs. The crowds roared at the sight of blood and urged their favorites on to the death.

Telemachus couldn't stand it. He knew it was wrong; this wasn't the way God wanted people to live or to die. So little Telemachus worked his way through the crowds to the wall down by the arena. "In the name of Christ, forbear!" he shouted.

Nobody heard him, so he crawled onto the wall and shouted again: "In the name of Christ, forbear!" This time the few who heard him only laughed. But Telemachus was not to be ignored. He jumped into the arena and ran through the sands toward the gladiators. "In the name of Christ, forbear!"

The crowds laughed at the silly little man and threw stones at him. Telemachus, however, was on a mission. He threw himself between two gladiators to stop their fighting. "In the name of Christ, forbear!" he cried.

They hacked him apart! They cut his body from shoulder to stomach, and he fell onto the sand with the life running out of his body.

The gladiators were stunned and stopped to watch him die. Then the crowds fell back in silence, and, for a moment, no one in the Coliseum moved. Telemachus' final words rang in their memories: "In the name of Christ, forbear!" At last they moved, slowly at first, but growing in numbers. The masses of Rome filed out of the Coliseum that day, and the historian Theodoret reports that never again was a gladiator contest held there! All because of the witness and the testimony of a single Christian who had the glow-in-the-dark power of grace and God's goodness.

During the time of the Reformation, John Foxe of England was impressed by the testimony of the early Christians. He delved into the pages of early historical writings and wrote a book that has become a classic in the church, *Foxe's Book of Martyrs*.

One story is about an early church leader named Lawrence. Lawrence acted as a pastor for a church community. He also collected the offerings for the poor each week.

A band of thieves found out that Lawrence received the offerings of the people from Sunday to Sunday, so one night, as he was out taking a stroll, they grabbed him and demanded the money. He told them that he didn't have it and had already given the offering to the poor. They didn't believe him and told him they would give him a chance to find it. In three days they would come to his house and take from him the treasures of the church.

Three days later they did come but Lawrence wasn't alone. The house was filled with the people of his congregation. When the thieves demanded the treasures of the church, Lawrence smiled. He opened wide his arms and gestured to those who sat around him. "Here's the treasure of the church!" he said. "Here's the treasure of God that shines in the world!"

Indeed. As Jesus said in another place, "You are the light of the world." You can glow in the dark of this world, shining the light of the transfiguration to those who desperately need it. Amen.

## *If You Like This Book...*

Wayne Brouwer has also written **Humming Till The Music Returns**, Second Lesson Sermons for Advent/Christmas/Epiphany, Cycle B (978-0-7880-1506-9) (printed book $17.95, e-book $9.95).

He has also contributed to **Sermons on the Gospel Readings**, Series II, Cycle A, the middle third section of Pentecost titled "Political Religion" (978-0-7880-2453-5) (printed book $37.95, e-book $29.95).

## *Other Cycle C Advent/Christmas/Epiphany Lectionary Titles...*

**The Presence in the Promise**
Harry Huxhold
978-0-7880-1713-1
printed book $14.95 / e-book $9.95

**Praying for a Whole New World**
William Carter
978-0-7880-1728-5
printed book $14.95 / e-book $9.95

contact CSS Publishing Company, Inc.
www.csspub.com          800-241-4056

Prices are subject to change without notice.

**Deep Joy for a Shallow World**
Richard Wing
978-0-7880-1033-0
printed book $15.95 / e-book $9.95

**Where Is God in All This?**
Tony Everett
978-0-7880-1028-6
printed book $12.95 / e-book $9.95

**The Days Are Surely Coming**
Robert Hausman
978-0-7880-0025-6
printed book $12.95 / e-book $9.95

contact CSS Publishing Company, Inc.
www.csspub.com          800-241-4056

Prices are subject to change without notice.

www.ingramcontent.com/pod-product-compliance
Lightning Source LLC
Chambersburg PA
CBHW071723040426
42446CB00011B/2192